MAS... INCLUSIVE LEADERSHIP

- Practical Strategies for Team Building and Retention
- Fostering Psychological Safety
- Employing Emotional Intelligence
- Transforming Workplaces by Advancing Diversity, Equity, and Inclusion

Mr. Grant T. Harris, MBA, CDE®

Viking Publications of Tennessee

Mastering Inclusive Leadership

Practical Strategies for Team Building and Retention, Fostering Psychological Safety, Employing Emotional Intelligence, Transforming Workplaces by Advancing Diversity, Equity, and Inclusion

© 2024, Grant T. Harris & Viking Publications of Tennessee.
All rights reserved.
Published by Viking Publications of Tennessee
463 East Parkway
Gatlinburg, TN 37738

No part of this publication may be reproduced, distributed, or transmitted in any form or by any means, including photocopying, recording, or other electronic or mechanical methods, without the prior written permission of the publisher, except in the case of brief quotations embodied in critical reviews and certain other noncommercial uses permitted by copyright law. This book is a work of non-fiction. Any resemblance to actual events, locales, or persons, living or dead, is entirely coincidental.

Cataloging-in-Publication Data for this book is available from the Library of Congress.

ISBN: 9798324282714

Printed in the United States.

First Edition: April 2024

Cover & Interior Design by Viking Publications of Tennessee

For information regarding special discounts for bulk purchases, please contact Viking Publications of Tennessee Special Sales at 463 East Tennessee, Gatlinburg, TN 37738

LIMIT OF LIABILITY/DISCLAIMER OF WARRANTY: The publisher and the author make no representations or warranties with respect to the accuracy or completeness of the contents of this work and specifically disclaim all warranties, including without limitation warranties of fitness for a particular purpose. No warranty may be created or extended by sales or promotional materials. The advice and strategies contained herein may not be suitable for every situation.

This work is sold with the understanding that the publisher is not engaged in rendering legal, accounting, or other professional services. If professional assistance is required, the services of a competent professional person should be sought. Neither the publisher nor the author shall be liable for damages arising herefrom. The fact that an organization or website is referred to in this work as a citation and/or a potential source of further information does not mean that the author or the publisher endorses the information the organization or website may provide or recommendations it may make.

Mastering Inclusive Leadership

Table of Contents

Introduction 8

Chapter 1

Setting the Stage. 13

Section 1: A Beacon of Inclusivity: Sodexo's Winning Strategy 13

Section 2: Understanding DEI: The Bedrock of Business Brilliance. 14

Section 3: Dispelling Shadows: Busting DEI Myths 18

Section 4: Reflecting Within: Assessing Your Current DEI Status 20

Section 5: Interpreting the Findings: Understanding DEI Metrics 23

Section 6: The Journey Ahead: Embracing DEI for a Brighter Future 24

Chapter 2

Enhancing Self-Perception 29

Section 1: Illuminating Leadership: A Case Study of Kaiser Permanente's DEI Strategy 29

Section 2: The Mirror of Leadership: Understanding the Need for Self-Awareness 31

Section 3: Beyond the Surface: Recognizing Your Biases 33

Section 4: Emotional Acumen in Leadership 35

Section 5: Cultural Adaptability: Embracing Diversity in Thought and Action 37

Section 6: From Reflection to Action: The DEI Leader's Toolkit 40

Section 7: Bringing It All Together: A Prelude to Inclusive Teams 42

Chapter 3

Crafting Cohesion........................ 51

Section 1: A Beacon of Inclusivity - Ernst & Young's (EY) Trailblazing Approach 51

Section 2: Strategies for Inclusive Recruitment, Onboarding, and Retention 53

Section 3: Building a Welcoming Team from Day One........ 56

Section 4: Keeping Talent Through Ongoing Development ... 58

Section 5: Championing Retention Through Inclusive Practices 60

Chapter 4

Validating Safe Spaces..................... 67

Section 1: Empowering Safe and Open Work Environments .. 67

Section 2: The Essence of Psychological Safety in the Workplace 70

Section 3: The Impact of Psychological Safety Stages on Workers and Workplaces... 72

Section 4: Building Psychological Safety at Work 74

Section 5: Establishing Fairness Through Policy.............. 75

Section 6: The Interplay of Psychological Safety, Communication, and Policy: Acknowledging Challenges..................... 77

Chapter 5

Embodying Authentic Leadership 85

Section 1: Building Genuine Leadership in Diverse Environments 85

Section 2: Innovative Integration of DEI in Corporate Culture: Understanding Slack's Approach to DEI..................... 87

Section 3: The Real You: Embracing Authentic Leadership.... 89

Section 4: The Positive Butterfly Effect of Authentic Leadership 91

Section 5: The Limitations of Authentic Leadership.......... 92

Chapter 6

Recognizing and Navigating Challenges 101

Section 1: Introduction: Charting a Course Through Resistance in DEI Initiatives... 101

Section 2: Embracing Diversity for Organizational Success .. 102

Section 3: Benefits of a Diverse and Inclusive Environment.. 103

Section 4: Spotting Roadblocks: How to Understand Obstacles 105

Section 5: Change the Course: Strategies to Overcome Skepticism 108

Section 6: Keep the Ball Rolling: How to Maintain DEI Efforts Over Time 111

Section 7: Recap of Chapter 6: Navigating the DEI Landscape 112

Chapter 7

Applying Theory 119

Section 1: Cisco's Robust DEI Framework - A Model of Success 119

Section 2: Wins Worth Sharing - Real Success Stories in DEI Training 123

Section 3: Your DEI Toolbox - Inclusive Leadership Toolkit.. 125

Section 4: Make It Fit - Tailoring DEI Training to Your Context 129

Chapter 8

Envisioning the Future 135

Section 1: Innovative Leadership at Apple: A Closer Look at DEI

Strategy. 135

Section 2: Getting Ready for the Future: Getting Prepared for Evolving Trends in Diversity, Equity and Inclusion 137

Section 3: Looking Beyond Boundaries: Getting Ready for Global Influence. 137

Section 4: Current Developments Influencing Diversity, Equity and Inclusion 138

Section 5: Tailoring Training Programs for Upcoming DEI Trends. 139

Section 6: Wrapping up Chapter 8 with a Call to Action 140

Conclusion. 146

Introduction

"Breaking the Mold: Pioneering Inclusion for Organizational Excellence"

"The path to diversity begins with supporting, mentoring, and sponsoring diverse women and men to become leaders and entrepreneurs."

– Denise Morrison, Former CEO of Campbell Soup Company

Picture this scenario: You walk into a boardroom armed with a game-changing proposal, only to be met with a homogeneous group that mirrors not the world's diversity but a narrow segment. This lack of diversity isn't just a discomfort; it's a blatant sign that something is amiss. It may catch your attention to know that 67% of job seekers consider a company's diversity when making employment decisions (Bonusly, n.d.), and over half the current workforce desires more vigorous strides in diversity from their employers (Pew Research Center, 2023).

The heart of the issue extends beyond mere personal discomfort to the crux of organizational potential. This speaks to the loss of rich, multifaceted dialogues and the innovative potential that arises from diverse collective intelligence. Suppose the constriction of uniformity or the underutilization of varied talents due to non-inclusive practices has been a point of contention for you. In that case, you understand there's a divide to be bridged between the current reality and the potential of what your organization could achieve.

Your choice to engage with this book reflects an understanding that real change stems from more than just grand visions; it comes from systematically applying insights, actions, and commitments that collectively redefine the norm. You're searching for the "how" — the methods and steps that translate into tangible progress, the kind that moves values from paper into practice. Herein, you'll find a toolkit designed for building a vibrant organizational culture rich with diversity, equity, and inclusion.

Introduction

DEI Strategy	Action Steps	Goals
Inclusive Culture Initiation	• Review and adjust company policies • Ensure diverse decision-making panels • Conduct regular culture evaluations	Develop a work environment that mirrors societal diversity in all business operations.
Self-Awareness Enhancement	• Introduce bias awareness workshops • Promote personal reflection exercises • Supply resources for ongoing education	Equip personnel with the insight to identify and rectify unconscious biases in themselves and others.
Diversity Engagement in Talent Management	• Advertise jobs with inclusive language • Start mentorship programs for career growth • Offer benefits catering to diverse demographics	Build and sustain a varied workforce that thrives within the company's environment.
DEI Adversity Response	• Develop a plan for DEI resistance • Facilitate open forums for input and dialogue • Provide education on DEI advantages	Ready the company to effectively confront and convert challenges to DEI policies into collaborative support.
Leadership Adaptability	• Keep abreast of DEI updates and changes • Network with DEI thought leaders • Reevaluate leadership practices annually	Position leadership to be aware of and responsive to the evolving landscape of workplace diversity and inclusion.

Mastering Inclusive Leadership

These strategies are not theoretical musings but tried-and-tested paths endorsed by leaders across the spectrum of industry who have witnessed their power to reshape the cultural contours of their organizations. After adopting these principles, they have observed the following impacts: amplified innovation, increased job satisfaction, and measurable business success.

Imagine a workplace where diversity is not just represented but is integral to its operational success; a haven for talent to flourish and contribute fully. This book serves as the road map for such an organizational ecosystem, pointing the way to a future where diversity will be a strength.

Previously, the road to embedding DEI within corporate culture may have seemed fraught with insurmountable challenges. However, armed with these pages' knowledge and success stories, that path is now well-lit and ready to travel. This guide is for you, the professional poised to enrich your organization with diversity, to champion a culture of equity, and to celebrate the inclusivity that drives market-leading innovation. It is for the decision-makers who recognize that to excel in a competitive market; an organization must be as diverse in thought as it is in its demographic makeup.

Welcome to the definitive resource for the professional ready to embrace the future. You are poised to be part of the change that sees diversity, equity, and inclusion as not only beneficial but essential for organizational excellence. This book is more than just a call to action—it's a proven playbook for those ready to move from Compliance (I/Me) to **Community** (We/Us). Let's take the ride together. **#WeNotMe**

References

1. Bonusly. (n.d.). Diversity & Inclusion Statistics. Retrieved from https://bonusly.com/post/diversity-inclusion-statistics
2. Pew Research Center. (2023, May 17). Diversity, Equity, and Inclusion in the Workplace. Retrieved from https://www.pewresearch.org/social-trends/2023/05/17/diversity-equity-and-inclusion-in-the-workplace/
3. Built In. (n.d.). Diversity in the Workplace Statistics. Retrieved from https://builtin.com/diversity-inclusion/diversity-in-the-workplace-statistics

Mastering Inclusive Leadership

Chapter 1
Setting the Stage

Section 1: A Beacon of Inclusivity: Sodexo's Winning Strategy

"We are convinced that our differences make the difference."

- Denis Machuel, CEO of Sodexo

Sodexo stands out as a shining example of inclusive excellence in a world that increasingly values what businesses do and how they do it. The French food services and facilities management giant has taken bold strides in embedding diversity, equity, and inclusion (DEI) into its core strategic vision, recognizing that a broad range of perspectives is vital for enduring success.

The Sodexo Story: An Inclusive Culture by Design

At Sodexo, diversity is not just a buzzword; it's a business imperative. With a presence in 80 countries and catering to a myriad of clients with diverse needs and backgrounds, Sodexo has made an unwavering commitment to reflect this diversity within its workforce. But, their holistic approach sets them apart - pioneering initiatives that span gender balance, cultural diversity, disability inclusion, and LGBTQ+ advocacy. Sodexo's DEI strategy is as comprehensive as it is impactful.

There have been several admirable milestones along their path to inclusive prosperity. The company's leadership has endorsed programs encouraging hiring from underrepresented groups, fostered a work environment that allows all employees to thrive, and implemented training to minimize unconscious bias. It's a strategy that resonates with both the moral and market imperatives of our times.

Mastering Inclusive Leadership

Charting Success: Sodexo's DEI Milestones

- **Gender Balance:** Sodexo's commitment to gender-balanced leadership saw women occupying 55% of the group's board positions as of 2021, a figure well above the global corporate average.
- **Cultural Diversity:** With operations worldwide, Sodexo leverages its global footprint to nurture a culturally diverse and sensitive workforce.
- Disability Inclusion: Recognized as a top employer for people with disabilities, Sodexo ensures accessible workplaces and supportive policies.
- **LGBTQIA+ Advocacy:** Sodexo's active support for LGBTQIA+ employees has earned it a spot on the Bloomberg Gender-Equality Index.

The results speak volumes. Sodexo's dedicated DEI efforts have earned it accolades and awards and contributed to robust financial performance and essential employee and customer satisfaction levels. This narrative affirms that when companies invest in DEI, they are not just doing good—they're doing well.

Section 2: Understanding DEI: The Bedrock of Business Brilliance

The DEI Triad Explained

Before delving deeper into the intricacies of DEI, it is essential to dismantle the concepts and lay a clear foundation for understanding.

- Diversity refers to the presence of differences within a given setting. This encompasses race, ethnicity, gender, age, religion, disability, sexual orientation, education, and national origin, among other differentiators.
- Equity is the process of ensuring fair treatment, equality of opportunity, and fairness in access to information and resources for all.
- Inclusion is the practice of creating environments in which any person or group can feel welcomed, respected, supported, and valued enough to participate fully.

Setting the Stage

An organization reaping the benefits of DEI is like a garden thriving with a wide variety of plants: each adds unique beauty and contributes to the ecosystem's health. Just as a gardener would tend to each plant's needs, an inclusive leader must cultivate an environment where every person can flourish.

DEI in Societal and Business Contexts

While DEI is a social concept at its heart, its relevance extends far beyond the reach of moral obligation into the realm of business excellence. Inclusivity breeds innovation, equity engenders loyalty, and diversity drives profitability.

Societal Impacts of DEI

DEI programs are not merely charitable gestures but investments in social stability and progress. They influence communities by fostering social cohesion and increasing economic participation. By elevating marginalized voices and breaking down systemic barriers, DEI initiatives contribute to a more just society.

Business Advantages of DEI

In the corporate world, DEI's benefits are manifold. A diverse workforce mirrors a global customer base, allowing for more profound insights and connections. Equity ensures that talent is harnessed effectively, regardless of background. Inclusion leads to a collaborative and innovative work environment, a prerequisite for outperforming competitors in today's dynamic market.

The DEI Business Case in Numbers

- **Profitability:** Companies with more diverse management teams have 19% higher revenue due to innovation (Boston Consulting Group, 2018).
- **Performance:** Organizations with above-average gender diversity and employee engagement outperform companies with below-average diversity by 58% (Gallup, 2014).
- **Innovation:** Diverse companies are 1.7 times more likely to be innovation leaders in their market segments (Forbes, 2021).

Mastering Inclusive Leadership

The DEI Effect

Element	Definition	Importance	Actionable Steps	Counterpoints or Counterexamples
Diversity	The presence of differences within a given setting, encompassing race, ethnicity, gender, etc.	Fosters innovation and reflects global markets.	Encourage diverse hiring practices and support diverse leadership development.	Some argue that diversity may lead to conflict or slow decision-making due to varying perspectives (Homan et al., 2007).
Equity	Fair treatment, access, opportunity, and advancement for all people while striving to identify and eliminate barriers.	Promotes fairness and justice in opportunities.	Implement policies that actively redress imbalances in opportunity and access.	Equity efforts can be perceived as favoritism or reverse discrimination, especially when poorly communicated (Kaiser et al., 2013).
Inclusion	Creating environments where any individual or group can be and feel welcomed, respected, supported, and valued to participate fully.	Enhances engagement and employee satisfaction.	Promote inclusive culture through training and awareness initiatives.	Inclusion initiatives may be met with resistance if seen as tokenistic or if they need to address underlying systemic issues (Dobbin and Kalev, 2016).

The Ripple Effect: DEI's Impact on Society and Enterprise

Forging Social Fabric: DEI's Role in Community Building

When diversity, equity, and inclusion become woven into the societal fabric, communities transform. People from all walks of life begin to experience a sense of belonging and participation, leading to a more vibrant and dynamic community life. This transformation uplifts individuals and creates a ripple effect that benefits all layers of society by enhancing social capital, encouraging civic participation, and fostering economic empowerment.

Setting the Stage

- **Social Cohesion:** Inclusive societies experience less conflict and more social stability.
- **Economic Participation:** Equity in access to education and jobs drives overall economic growth by maximizing every citizen's potential.

The Corporate Growth Engine: How DEI Fuels Business

In the business sphere, DEI is not just a catalyst for social good but a powerhouse for economic performance. Integrating DEI principles drives companies to new heights of innovation, customer satisfaction, and financial success.

- **Employee Satisfaction:** A workplace that values all employees' contributions sees higher levels of job satisfaction and lower turnover rates.
- **Customer Relations:** A diverse business is better equipped to understand and meet the needs of a diverse client base.
- **Profitability:** A commitment to DEI correlates with better financial outcomes, as a more diverse and inclusive workforce is more adept at problem-solving and creativity.

Including different perspectives, especially from underrepresented groups, brings forth an array of ideas and solutions that might otherwise be overlooked. This variety is the seedbed of innovation, allowing businesses to anticipate market needs and adapt to changes more swiftly.

Statistical Showcase: DEI's Business Benefits

- **Talent Pool Expansion:** Companies that champion DEI tap into a broader talent pool, driving competition and elevating the quality of their workforce.
- **Engagement and Trust:** Firms with inclusive cultures see a 20% increase in employee engagement (Deloitte, 2015).
- **Innovative Mindsets:** Businesses with diverse teams have a 35% higher likelihood of outperforming their peers (McKinsey, 2015).
- **Decision Making:** Diverse teams are 87% better at decision-making processes (Cloverpop, 2017).

Mastering Inclusive Leadership

- **Performance and Profits:** Organizations with high racial and ethnic diversity are 35% more likely to have financial returns above their national industry medians (McKinsey, 2015).

DEI's Quantifiable Gains

Impact Area	Evidence or Data Point	Business Benefit	Actionable Steps	Counterpoints or Counterexamples
Social Impact	DEI programs can drive community development and social cohesion (Region Five, n.d.).	Reflects social responsibility and improves brand image.	Support community-based DEI efforts and partnerships.	Critics suggest that focusing on social impacts may divert resources from core business functions (Friedman, 1970).
Employee Satisfaction	Companies with DEI are 1.7 times more likely to be innovation leaders in their market (Deloitte, 2013).	Attracts top talent and promotes a competitive edge.	Create mentorship programs and career development plans inclusive of diverse employees.	Some employees may feel that DEI programs create undue pressure to conform to new norms (Plaut, 2010).
Profitability and Performance	Diverse companies are 33% more likely to outperform on profitability (McKinsey & Company, 2015).	Higher profitability and market share	Conduct regular DEI training and ensure diverse representation in decision-making roles.	Overemphasis on DEI can lead to neglecting other key performance drivers like operational efficiency (Bloom and Van Reenen, 2010).

Section 3: Dispelling Shadows: Busting DEI Myths

Myth-Busting: Separating DEI Facts from Fiction

Myth: DEI Is a Zero-Sum Game

The misconception that advancing one group's interests must come at the expense of another persists stubbornly. However, DEI's premise is not competition but expansion. DEI initiatives add to the collective pot by creating more opportunities for all rather than redistributing existing resources.

Setting the Stage

Myth: DEI Is Only a Human Resources Issue

Some believe DEI is confined to the HR department, but it's a strategic element of business that influences all areas, from marketing to product development to customer service. DEI is a leadership issue, a market issue, and a creativity and innovation issue.

Myth: DEI Efforts Are Just Corporate Window-Dressing

While there may be instances of performative allyship, genuine DEI efforts are deeply rooted in organizational strategy and have tangible impacts on business outcomes. They go beyond public relations to reshape company culture and operational effectiveness.

Myth: Focusing on DEI Limits Meritocracy

Meritocracy and DEI are not mutually exclusive. In fact, DEI initiatives aim to ensure that meritocracy is genuinely based on ability by removing unconscious biases and structural barriers that prevent the best talent from rising to the top, irrespective of their background.

Evidence in the Light: The Truth About DEI

- **Increased Resource Pool:** DEI expands the 'pie' by leveraging the full spectrum of human talent and creativity (Harvard Business Review, 2016).

- **Cross-Functional Impact:** DEI enhances performance across all business functions, not just HR (Deloitte Insights, 2017).

- **Authentic Integration:** Companies with authentic DEI integration see 2.3 times higher cash flow per employee over three years (Center for Talent Innovation, 2017).

- **Enhanced Meritocracy:** DEI practices lead to a more competitive workforce by ensuring opportunities are accessible to the most deserving based on their capabilities (McKinsey, 2018).

Mastering Inclusive Leadership

Deconstructing DEI Myths and Realities

Impact Area	Evidence or Data Point	Business Benefit	Actionable Steps	Counterpoints or Counterexamples
Social Impact	DEI programs can drive community development and social cohesion (Region Five, n.d.).	Reflects social responsibility and improves brand image.	Support community-based DEI efforts and partnerships.	Critics suggest that focusing on social impacts may divert resources from core business functions (Friedman, 1970).
Employee Satisfaction	Companies with DEI are 1.7 times more likely to be innovation leaders in their market (Deloitte, 2013).	Attracts top talent and promotes a competitive edge.	Create mentorship programs and career development plans inclusive of diverse employees.	Some employees may feel that DEI programs create undue pressure to conform to new norms (Plaut, 2010).
Profitability and Performance	Diverse companies are 33% more likely to outperform on profitability (McKinsey & Company, 2015).	Higher profitability and market share	Conduct regular DEI training and ensure diverse representation in decision-making roles.	Overemphasis on DEI can lead to neglecting other key performance drivers like operational efficiency (Bloom and Van Reenen, 2010).

Section 4: Reflecting Within: Assessing Your Current DEI Status

The Starting Point: Knowing Your Baseline

To steer a ship in the right direction, one must know its starting position. Similarly, before an organization can progress on its DEI voyage, it must first understand its current standing. A DEI audit provides this baseline, clearly showing where a company excels and where it requires improvement.

Incorporating the R.A.C.E.™ Framework into DEI Audits

As organizations endeavor to gauge and enhance their DEI initiatives, the **R.A.C.E.™** framework emerges as a pivotal tool in illuminating the path

Setting the Stage

forward. This framework aligns with the audit process, providing a clear, actionable structure for organizations to follow.

1. **Recognize:** Initiate self-assessment to ascertain alignment between personal convictions and workplace habits. It urges introspection on whether daily activities resonate with individual and organizational values.

2. **Acknowledge:** Emphasize the responsibility of gauging the intention behind actions and their subsequent impact. It's not just about good intent; it's about ensuring that the outcomes align with those intentions.

3. **Cultivate:** Leaders and organizations are encouraged to delve deep into learning, gather data, and pinpoint areas of unawareness or blind spots. This is a call for inclusivity, ensuring diverse voices are integral to the decision-making process.

4. **Engage:** Transcend beyond mere words. It's a clarion call for genuine behavioral transformation, consistent action, and fostering a community-centric mindset that benefits society as a whole.

   - By recognizing their current state of DEI through self-assessment, leaders can compare their personal and company-wide practices with the benchmarks of inclusive excellence.

   - Not only does acknowledging DEI efforts mean agreeing with their good intentions, but it also means looking closely at the results to make sure they are in line with stated values.

   - The cultivation phase calls for a commitment to cultivate more profound understanding and awareness, seeking out blind spots in current strategies and inviting diverse voices to rectify them.

   - Lastly, engaging with these insights means translating them into decisive actions that effect genuine change and drive community growth rather than superficial compliance.

Through this four-step approach, the **R.A.C.E.™** framework can facilitate a company's proactive movement from awareness to meaningful action, propelling both internal progress and societal contribution.

Mastering Inclusive Leadership

Crafting the DEI Audit: A Step-by-Step Approach

A DEI audit involves a comprehensive review of policies, practices, and procedures to identify strengths and gaps in fostering an inclusive workplace. Here's how to initiate this introspective process:

1. **Leadership and Culture Assessment:** Evaluate the commitment of top leadership to DEI and the cultural norms that define the organization's inclusivity.
2. **Recruitment and Hiring Practices:** Scrutinize the fairness and effectiveness of recruitment and hiring processes.
3. **Employee Satisfaction and Retention:** Gauge employee sentiment and analyze retention rates with a focus on diverse group representation.
4. **Development and Advancement Opportunities:** Ensure equal opportunities for professional growth and advancement are available to all employees.
5. **External Community and Client Relations:** Consider the organization's image and engagement with diverse external stakeholders.

The Audit Toolkit: Gathering Qualitative and Quantitative Data

- **Surveys:** Collect employee perceptions of DEI within the organization.
- **Interviews:** Conduct discussions with employees across various levels to gain detailed insights.
- **Document Review:** Examine formal policies and procedures for DEI alignment.
- **Observation:** Assess everyday interactions and organizational practices.

Section 5: Interpreting the Findings: Understanding DEI Metrics

Once the data is gathered, interpreting it requires a balanced approach. Look for patterns that indicate systemic issues and celebrate areas of success. Red flags might include significant disparities in representation at different job levels, pronounced dissatisfaction in minority groups, or a lack of DEI awareness among staff.

Conducting a DEI Audit

Audit Area	Tools for Assessment	Indicators of Success	Actionable Steps	Counterpoints or Counterexamples
Leadership & Culture	Surveys, Leadership Interviews	Alignment of DEI values with leadership actions.	Train leaders in DEI principles; create DEI accountability metrics for leadership.	Some leaders may view DEI as a constraint on their decision-making authority (Ely and Thomas, 2001).
Recruitment & Hiring	Policy Analysis, Recruitment Data	Diversity in candidate pools and new hires.	Use blind recruitment processes; offer internships to underrepresented groups.	Blind recruitment processes can be critiqued for not addressing bias post-hire (Bohnet, 2016).
Employee Satisfaction & Retention	Employee Surveys, Turnover Statistics	High satisfaction scores, equitable retention rates.	Develop retention programs targeting diverse employee needs; conduct exit interviews to understand turnover causes.	Higher retention of diverse employees can be criticized for causing complacency (Phillips, 2014).
Development & Advancement	Promotion Data, Training Records	Equitable advancement opportunities, diverse leadership	Provide leadership development for underrepresented employees; ensure transparency in promotion decisions.	Others may view development initiatives that target particular groups as unfair (Castilla, 2008).

External Relations	Client Feedback, Community Engagement	Positive brand perception engages diverse stakeholders.	Engage in community DEI initiatives; ensure marketing campaigns reflect diversity.	Some external stakeholders may question the authenticity of DEI in marketing as pandering (Drumwright, 1996).

Section 6: The Journey Ahead: Embracing DEI for a Brighter Future

Conclusion: Laying the Foundation

In this opening chapter, we've navigated the fundamentals of DEI, the compelling case for its integration into society and business, and how to dispel common myths surrounding it. Sodexo's story was a concrete example of how robust DEI practices can propel a company to global success, fostering a work environment where every voice is heard and valued.

Preparing for the Next Steps: Anticipating Chapter 2

Understanding DEI is the first step toward inclusive leadership, but awareness alone is not enough. The subsequent phase of this exploration involves looking inward to recognize personal biases and improve emotional intelligence. Chapter 2 will guide readers through self-reflection and the cultivation of an inclusive mindset, setting the stage for practicing inclusive leadership in everyday actions. We'll unveil the transformative power of personal growth and enlightened leadership in creating a more inclusive world. Through introspection and commitment, leaders can shape an environment that not only embraces diversity but thrives on it in their pursuit of moving from Compliance (I/Me) to **Community** (We/Us)™ **#WeNotMe**.

Chapter One Takeaways

Key Areas	Summary of Takeaways
Sodexo's DEI Strategy	Sodexo demonstrates inclusive leadership by reflecting diversity within its workforce and pioneering DEI initiatives across various fronts.
DEI in Business	DEI is crucial for business innovation, equity engenders loyalty, and diversity drives profitability.

Setting the Stage

DEI Milestones	Sodexo and other companies have shown that DEI contributes to financial performance and high levels of employee and customer satisfaction.
DEI Audit	A DEI audit establishes an organization's baseline for inclusivity, identifying areas of success and opportunities for improvement.
Myth-Busting DEI	DEI is not a zero-sum game. It's not just an HR issue; it's more than corporate window-dressing and does not limit meritocracy.
Preparing for Change	The journey towards inclusive leadership is ongoing and requires regular introspection and commitment to DEI values.

References

1. Boston Consulting Group. (2018). How diverse leadership teams boost innovation.

   https://www.bcg.com/en-us/publications/2018/how-diverse-leadership-teams-boost-innovation

2. Cloverpop. (2017). Hacking diversity with inclusive decision-making.

   https://www.cloverpop.com/hacking-diversity-with-inclusive-decision-making-white-paper

3. Deloitte. (2015). The radical transformation of diversity and inclusion: The millennial influence.

   https://www2.deloitte.com/us/en/pages/about-deloitte/articles/radical-transformation-of-diversity-and-inclusion-millennial-influence.html

4. Deloitte Insights. (2017). Diversity and inclusion: The reality gap.

   https://www2.deloitte.com/us/en/insights/focus/human-capital-trends/2017/diversity-and-inclusion-at-the-workplace.html

5. Forbes. (2021). Why diversity, equity, and inclusion will be a top priority for businesses in the 21st century.

   https://www.forbes.com/sites/forbeshumanresourcescouncil/2021/01/13/why-diversity-equity-and-inclusion-will-be-a-top-priority-for-businesses-in-the-21st-century/

6. Gallup. (2014). State of the American workplace report.

   https://www.gallup.com/workplace/238085/state-american-workplace-report-2017.aspx

7. Harvard Business Review. (2016). Why diversity programs fail.

   https://hbr.org/2016/07/why-diversity-programs-fail

8. McKinsey & Company. (2015). Why diversity matters.

   https://www.mckinsey.com/business-functions/organization/our-insights/why-diversity-matters

9. McKinsey & Company. (2018). Delivering through diversity. https://www.mckinsey.com/business-functions/organization/our-insights/delivering-through-diversity

10. Center for Talent Innovation. (2017). The power of diversity metrics. https://www.talentinnovation.org/publication.cfm?publication=1340

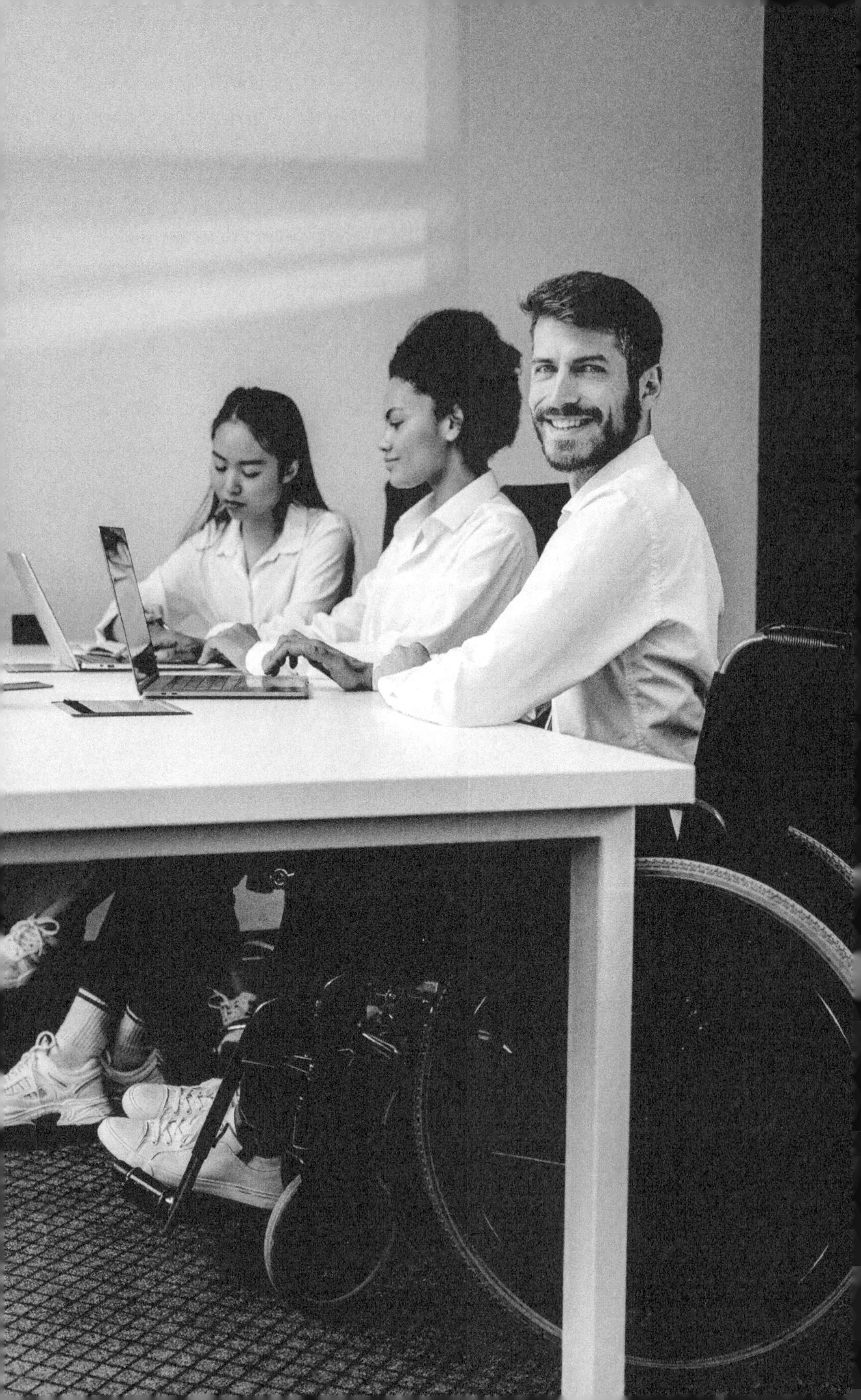

Chapter 2
Enhancing Self-Perception

Section 1: Illuminating Leadership: A Case Study of Kaiser Permanente's DEI Strategy

"He who knows others is wise; he who knows himself is enlightened."

– Lao Tzu

In a world where the demographic richness of the workforce is as varied as ever, Kaiser Permanente stands out as a leading example, demonstrating the power of a commitment to DEI. Kaiser Permanente has listened to the call for a diverse workforce and set an excellent example by aligning its company values with a strategic, all-encompassing DEI framework. This is because the healthcare system is as diverse as people are.

At Kaiser Permanente, the belief that a diverse organization is strong translates into a series of proactive programs and initiatives. Kaiser Permanente has set the stage for inclusive excellence with its National Diversity and Inclusion Strategy, which ties together workforce diversity, culturally competent care, and community health. The healthcare giant has also created targeted growth and development programs for employees from underrepresented groups. (Kaiser Permanente, 2022)

Programs and Outcomes

Kaiser Permanente's multifaceted approach includes leadership development programs, supplier diversity, and a commitment to health equity. These initiatives are designed to cater to a diverse clientele and carve out a

Mastering Inclusive Leadership

space where every member of the Kaiser Permanente family, irrespective of their background, can thrive. One such program, the "National Diversity and Inclusion Strategy," has been particularly effective in enabling an environment where different perspectives are welcomed and seen as crucial to innovation and problem-solving.

By integrating DEI into its operational strategy, Kaiser Permanente has realized tangible benefits, such as increased patient satisfaction and improved health outcomes in marginalized communities. The organization's inclusive policies have shown a ripple effect, enhancing employee morale and retention and establishing Kaiser Permanente as a leader in delivering equitable care (Glassdoor, 2022).

Kaiser Permanente's DEI Strategy and Success

DEI Strategy Element	Description	Outcomes Achieved	Actionable Steps for Other Organizations	Counterpoints Considered
Workforce Diversity	Recruitment and retention programs targeting underrepresented groups.	Increased diversity in staffing is reflective of patient demographics.	Implement similar recruitment initiatives to broaden talent acquisition.	A more diverse workforce may require enhanced conflict resolution skills (Johnson & Johnson, 2021).
Culturally Competent Care	Training and resources to provide care that respects patients' cultural backgrounds.	Higher patient satisfaction and better care outcomes in diverse populations.	Provide continuous cultural competence training for staff.	Overemphasis on cultural training can lead to stereotyping if not carefully managed (Health Affairs, 2018).
Community Health Initiatives	Partnerships and programs to address health disparities in communities	Improved community health statistics and reduced health disparities.	Engage in partnerships with local organizations to improve community health.	Initiatives may face challenges due to systemic issues beyond the scope of healthcare providers (Community Health Reports, 2020).

Section 2: The Mirror of Leadership: Understanding the Need for Self-Awareness

The Tale of a Leader's Awakening

In the competitive crucible of Silicon Valley, a tale unfolds of a leader at the helm of a pioneering tech company. They noticed a troubling trend: projects were stalling, and innovation, once the company's lifeblood, was waning. Initial assumptions pointed to external factors—market competition, technology shortfalls, perhaps team skill gaps. But the root cause was much closer to home. It was the leader's own unexamined biases that were casting a shadow over the team's potential.

A consultant was brought in, not to dissect the team's work but to hold up a mirror to the leadership's practices. What was revealed was a series of unconscious biases that shaped decisions in ways that stifled creativity and diversity of thought. This realization struck a chord, and the leader embarked on a personal quest for self-awareness, unlearning patterns that invisibly sabotaged their team's efficiency and morale.

Self-Awareness: The Heart of Understanding

Self-awareness is often the cornerstone of successful leadership. It is the conscious knowledge of one's character, feelings, motives, and desires. Leaders who possess a high degree of self-awareness can navigate complex interpersonal dynamics with finesse and align team efforts with broader organizational goals. They understand that leadership is not just about directive power but about understanding the unique composition of their team's skills and temperaments and leveraging these for collective success (BetterUp, n.d.).

Realizing one's mental and emotional blueprint allows leaders to channel their energy where it's needed most. It helps to temper responses to stress, mitigate conflict, and develop a genuine understanding of team morale. Self-awareness also plays a critical role in managing diversity within teams, equipping leaders with the sensitivity to recognize and respect varied perspectives and cultural nuances (Verywell Mind, n.d.).

The Peril of a Leader's Blind Spot

The absence of self-awareness in leadership can be likened to navigating a ship in foggy waters without radar; there's a high chance of going off course. When leaders operate with a lack of self-knowledge, they risk creating environments that are not conducive to openness and creativity. They may inadvertently impose their worldview on their team, stifling potential and innovation (Business News Daily, 2021).

This shortfall can manifest in several detrimental ways: poor decision-making, reduced employee engagement, and a culture of conformity rather than creativity. It can also result in a leader's inability to harness their team's full potential, as unrecognized biases may lead them to undervalue the contributions of specific team members.

Honing the Lens of Self-Perception

Leaders committed to increasing their self-awareness can adopt several strategies. They can begin with psychometric assessments to gain a baseline understanding of their personality traits and leadership styles. Engaging in regular, structured self-reflection—whether through journaling, mindfulness, or professional coaching—provides leaders with the feedback necessary for personal development (Forbes, 2018).

Structured reflection involves examining one's thought patterns, emotional reactions, and the subsequent impact on others. Mindfulness meditation trains the brain to focus on the present moment, offering clarity over one's mental state. Coaching, meanwhile, offers a structured and objective analysis of a leader's behavior, providing actionable insights and development plans.

Self-awareness also grows through encouraging diverse interactions outside one's comfort zone, seeking new perspectives, and engaging in continuous learning. In doing so, leaders broaden their understanding of others and expose themselves to different ways of thinking and being, which can challenge and refine their leadership approach.

By taking these steps, leaders can create a virtuous cycle of self-improvement and team enhancement, leading to a work environment where trust, innovation, and adaptability thrive. These practices are beneficial and essential in today's rapidly evolving and culturally diverse business landscape.

Enhancing Self-Perception

Navigating the Inner Leadership Landscape

The Inner Compass	Gaining Insight and Clarity	The Impact of Awareness	Pathways to Inner Clarity	The Other Side of the Mirror
Introspection	Engaging in self-reflection to better understand personal drivers and barriers.	More authentic decision-making aligns with true values.	Daily reflective practices like journaling or mindfulness	Risk of over-introspection leading to indecision or self-doubt.
Feedback Reception	Welcoming constructive criticism to refine leadership.	Increased adaptability and course-correction ability.	Creating a culture that values transparent feedback.	Potential for feedback overload or misinterpretation leading to confusion.
Emotional Awareness	Attuning to one's emotional state to manage interactions and responses.	Enhanced empathy and connection with team members.	Regular check-ins with self and others to gauge emotional climate.	Emotions in leadership may be misconstrued as weakness or volatility.
Coaching Engagement	Seeking external guidance to uncover blind spots.	Accelerated personal growth with impactful leadership insights.	Commitment to ongoing learning with a mentor or coach.	Coaching outcomes are dependent on the person's openness to change.

Section 3: Beyond the Surface: Recognizing Your Biases

The Unseen Influencers in Decision-Making

In the corridors of corporate power, daily decisions shape the future of companies and the careers of their employees. Leaders entrusted with this responsibility often believe they act on logic and meritocracy. Yet, beneath the surface of conscious thought, biases linger, influencing decisions with an invisible hand. A leader, for instance, reviewing candidates for a pivotal project may not realize how deeply their preference for a familiar background—like their own alma mater—impacts their choice. This inclination, known as affinity bias, is just one thread in the complex web of preconceived notions that can distort judgment and perpetuate homogeneity (Cleveland Clinic, 2021).

Mastering Inclusive Leadership

Unmasking the Hidden Gaze

Unconscious biases are cognitive shortcuts—the brain's attempt to make quick and efficient judgments based on past experiences and societal cues. They are the shadows that our previous interactions and cultural background have cast, which have colored our perception without our explicit consent. Biases can be based on race, gender, age, socioeconomic status, and a myriad of other social categories. They operate under the surface, subtly skewing the way leaders view talent and potential within their teams.

To confront these biases, leaders need to engage in the process of discovery and acknowledgment. Tools such as Implicit Association Tests and Self-assessment Questionnaires offer a starting point for recognizing these predispositions. By examining personal thought patterns and behaviors in a structured manner, leaders can identify the biases hindering their judgment and the organization's progress (Verywell Mind, 2023).

Illuminating Pathways Through Training

The process of addressing and mitigating bias is both enlightening and challenging. It involves conscious efforts to understand the roots of prejudice and develop strategies to counteract its effects. Training sessions designed to confront biases provide leaders with the space to explore their unconscious patterns and the tools to correct course.

Effective bias training challenges leaders to confront uncomfortable truths and embrace vulnerability as a step toward growth. Such training encourages a reflective pause in decision-making processes, prompting leaders to consider a fuller spectrum of data and perspectives. This critical introspection enables leaders to establish a workplace that truly values diversity and inclusive practices. Beyond just awareness, this training emboldens leaders to commit to continuous personal growth and to lead by example, setting a tone for their organizations that moves beyond compliance to genuine inclusivity (Harvard Business Review, 2021).

These strategies underscore the importance of reflective practice and education in leadership development. By actively engaging in the process of unlearning biases and relearning through a more inclusive lens, leaders can shape an environment that reflects the diverse world it serves. This commitment to equity and diversity goes beyond mere surface adjustments to profound structural change in organizational culture and practice.

Enhancing Self-Perception

The Unveiling of Bias in Leadership

Unearthing Bias	Description	Impact on Leadership	Strategy for Overcoming Bias	Beyond the Bias
Self-Assessment	Tools and tests to identify personal bias	More equitable and inclusive decision-making.	Use regular self-assessments to stay vigilant.	Risk of becoming too inward-focused and ignoring broader data.
Training Programs	Courses designed to educate about biases	Leadership that champions diversity and inclusion.	Mandatory bias training workshops for all leadership levels.	Training must translate into practical, measurable changes to be effective.
Continuous Learning	Ongoing education about bias.	A leadership style that evolves with new understanding.	Encourage attendance at DEI seminars and conferences.	Must balance the pursuit of learning with actionable leadership.
Policy Implementation	Establishing rules to govern fair practice	Creates a framework for accountability in decision-making	Develop clear policies that target bias reduction.	Policies can be circumvented if not deeply ingrained in company culture.

Section 4: Emotional Acumen in Leadership

The Emotional Pulse of an Organization

Leadership today goes far beyond strategic decision-making and administrative oversight. At its core, the essence of effective leadership is deeply tied to emotional acuity—the leader's proficiency in discerning the undercurrents of workplace dynamics, understanding the emotional needs of team members, and cultivating an atmosphere of mutual respect and understanding. Emotional intelligence (EQ) transcends the notion of 'soft skills' and emerges as a critical component in building resilient, adaptive, and high-performing teams. A leader with high EQ reads the room with finesse and influences the emotional climate positively, creating ripples that can turn the tide in favor of organizational well-being (HelpGuide, 2021).

Enriching Leadership with Emotional Depth

To enhance their emotional depth, leaders must dive into the realm of introspection and interaction with intent and attention. Practices contributing to this depth include active listening, a non-judgmental presence, and a commitment to understanding diverse emotional landscapes. Leaders must strive to understand what is being communicated and how it's being expressed—the stress in a voice, the hesitation before answering, the non-verbal cues that speak volumes.

For example, engaging in reflective practices such as mindfulness can sharpen a leader's attention to these details, cultivating a more nuanced engagement with their teams. Leaders can also benefit from training workshops focused on emotional intelligence, where they learn the significance of emotional feedback and the art of responding rather than reacting. This continuous learning process demands a persistent commitment to growth and learning (Harvard Business School Online, 2021).

Case Studies in Emotional Leadership

The landscape of leadership success stories is dotted with instances of emotional intelligence playing a pivotal role. A CEO's ability to navigate complex mergers with an empathetic approach towards employee anxieties, or a manager's skillful handling of a potentially explosive whistleblower incident, showcases EQ in action.

The adoption of EQ-centric leadership practices can be transformative. For instance, a leader at a technology firm implemented 'emotional check-ins' at the start of meetings, which led to improved team morale and increased productivity. Another leader, by acknowledging their anxiety during organizational changes, nurtured a culture of trust and openness that allowed for smoother transitions (Pagely, 2021).

These stories underscore the powerful impact of emotional intelligence on a leader's influence. By valuing and developing their emotional capabilities, leaders can create an environment where employees feel heard, valued, and motivated—a climate where the emotional well-being of every member is as vital as their professional success.

Enhancing Self-Perception

Sculpting the Emotional Intelligence of a Leader

Emotional Mastery	Description	Leadership Impact	Enhancement Techniques	Emotional Intelligence: A Double-Edged Sword
Active Listening	Full engagement in the communication process.	Stimulates trust and openness in teams.	Practice reflective listening and mindfulness.	Active listening requires time and patience, which may be in short supply in high-pressure situations.
Empathy Development	The ability to understand and share the feelings of another	Encourages a supportive environment conducive to growth.	Use role-playing exercises to understand diverse perspectives.	Misplaced empathy can lead to biased decisions favoring one group over another.
Emotional Regulation Training	Techniques to manage and respond to an emotional experience with a measured approach.	Reduces conflict and enhances leadership presence.	Engage in stress management and emotional regulation workshops.	Emotion regulation can be misinterpreted as emotional detachment or lack of passion.
Success Reflection	Analyzing successful outcomes to understand the role of emotional intelligence in achieving them.	Reinforces the value of EQ in practical settings.	Review case studies and personal experiences to identify EQ's benefits.	Success stories can oversimplify the complexity of leadership challenges and the role of EQ.

Section 5: Cultural Adaptability: Embracing Diversity in Thought and Action

The Symphony of Cultures

In the vibrant concert of today's workplace, cultural adaptability is the skill that ensures harmony among diverse notes. It's about understanding and valuing the rich array of backgrounds each team member brings to the table. When a leader excels in cultural adaptability, they conduct the ensemble of their team with respect and inclusivity, integrating different cultural expressions into a cohesive and effective unit. The result is a workplace environment that, like an orchestra, blends individual contributions into a collective performance that is greater than the sum of its parts.

Leaders who master cultural adaptability are adept at aligning varied cultural expressions with organizational goals. They create an inclusive atmosphere where diversity is accepted and celebrated as a source of innovation and strength. Such leaders are not just conductors but composers, capable of writing new narratives that include multiple perspectives and voices.

Cultural Adaptability: The Leader's Lingua Franca

For leaders to thrive in a global marketplace, cultural adaptability must be woven into the very fabric of their leadership style. It's about becoming fluent in the nuances of cultural diversity and developing a keen understanding of how cultural differences can impact teamwork and decision-making.

Leaders with a high degree of cultural adaptability are skilled at decoding and bridging cultural nuances. They recognize that effective communication goes beyond language barriers and extends into the subtler realms of context, meaning, and nonverbal expression. By supporting an environment where different cultural norms are acknowledged and respected, these leaders build robust, dynamic, and innovative teams.

Training for a World Stage

Cultural adaptability doesn't come naturally; it is honed through deliberate and thoughtful training. Leaders can start by reflecting on their cultural assumptions and learning how these biases shape their worldviews. Engaging with diverse groups and seeking understanding through dialogue and shared experiences are also key steps in this training.

Organizations may offer workshops on cultural intelligence, provide resources for learning about different cultural practices, and encourage participation in events that celebrate diversity. By adopting a learner's mindset, leaders can break down barriers that hinder collaboration and discover new ways to lead effectively in a global context.

Training for cultural adaptability means adopting an open-minded approach to learning and integrating diverse cultural insights into everyday practice. It's about moving from mere coexistence to genuine collaboration,

Enhancing Self-Perception

where the unique attributes of each culture are leveraged to achieve common goals.

Leaders can further this adaptability by actively seeking diverse mentors and role models, participating in cross-cultural networking events, and continuously challenging their cultural preconceptions. In doing so, they not only evolve their leadership skills but also contribute to building a corporate culture that is diverse, inclusive, and adaptable, ready to meet the challenges and opportunities of a rapidly changing world.

The Compass of Cultural Adaptability

Heading: Uniting Diverse Voices	Description	Leadership Significance	Adaptive Strategies	The Paradox of Adaptability
Cross-Cultural Communication	Engaging effectively with diverse cultures.	Bridges gaps, builds trust, and enhances collaboration.	Language training, diversity workshops, and team-building exercises	Risk of over-generalizing cultures or stereotyping.
Reflexive Practice	Continual self-examination of cultural biases and assumptions	Keeps leadership dynamic and responsive to change.	Regular diversity audits and feedback loops within teams	The challenge of balancing global outlooks with local nuances
Diversity Advocacy	Actively promoting and supporting diversity initiatives.	Positions leaders as role models for inclusivity.	Public commitment to diversity goals and measures of accountability.	Advocacy can become tokenistic if not backed up by sincere understanding and action.
Inclusivity Drills	Practice scenarios to encourage inclusive behavior.	Prepares leaders for real-world diversity challenges.	Role-play various cultural interactions and conflict-resolution scenarios.	Drills must be followed by actual, inclusive policy-making and implementation.

Section 6: From Reflection to Action: The DEI Leader's Toolkit

Equipping Leaders for the DEI Crusade

Leaders are the vanguard in the quest for a genuinely inclusive workplace, setting the tone for their organization's culture and values. An effective DEI Leader's Toolkit empowers these leaders to move beyond mere compliance to develop a thriving ecosystem where diversity is the cornerstone of innovation and productivity. This comprehensive toolkit offers more than guidelines—it provides a framework for understanding, a platform for growth, and a catalyst for change.

A leader equipped with this toolkit notifies the team that diversity goes beyond surface-level characteristics and taps into a wealth of perspectives, skills, and experiences. They learn to wield these tools not as a formality but as essential instruments in crafting a forward-thinking and resilient organization.

Self-Reflection: The First Tool

For leaders, the journey to DEI mastery starts with looking inward. Self-reflection is a pivotal tool that unpacks personal belief systems and uncovers hidden biases. This tool encourages leaders to question the status quo and the influence of their background on their leadership style.

Leaders are encouraged to adopt reflective practices routinely, carving out time for introspection amidst their busy schedules. Leaders can gain an understanding of how others perceive their actions and decisions through tools like self-assessment quizzes, 360-degree feedback, and personal coaching, enabling more inclusive and empathic leadership.

Emotional Intelligence (EQ): The Keystone of Interaction

Emotional intelligence is the essence of human interaction and is indispensable for a leader's toolkit. EQ enables leaders to read between the lines of spoken communication, understand the undercurrents of team morale, and respond to challenges with a blend of rationality and sensitivity.

By prioritizing EQ development, leaders can master the art of emotional conversation—listening to understand rather than respond, recognizing their team's emotional needs, and responding to workplace stress with compassion

Enhancing Self-Perception

and composure. Training in EQ cultivates an environment where emotional well-being is as critical as professional achievement.

Inclusive Mindset: Shaping the Lens of Leadership

An inclusive mindset is transformative, reshaping how leaders perceive their role and the impact they can have on their organization's culture. It's about adopting a worldview that sees diversity as a wellspring of creativity and a driving force for business success.

Leaders with an inclusive mindset engage in continuous learning about different cultures, identities, and life experiences. They promote policies and practices that ensure equal opportunity for all and actively dismantle barriers that prevent full participation. Cultivating this mindset is not a passive process; it requires leaders to become champions for change, advocating for diversity within their teams and throughout their entire organization.

A leader's commitment to an inclusive mindset extends beyond their teams—it influences supplier choices, partnership opportunities, and community relations. This proactive stance on diversity and inclusion becomes a defining trait of the organization, attracting talent, partnerships, and customers who share these values.

By integrating these tools into their daily practices, leaders can move from reflection to action and from intention to impact. The DEI Leader's Toolkit is designed to be dynamic, evolving with the leader's growth and the organization's shifting landscapes. With each tool comes the responsibility to apply it wisely and the opportunity to drive meaningful change.

The Leader's DEI Toolkit

Toolkit Component	Application in Leadership	Impact on the Organizational Culture	Action Steps for Leaders	The Cautionary Notes
Self-Reflection	Understanding the personal impact on team dynamics.	Creates a foundation for trust and mutual respect.	Engage in regular self-assessment and solicit feedback.	Beware of navel-gazing that does not lead to actionable change.

EQ Training	Enhancing interpersonal skills and emotional responsiveness.	Cultivates a culture of empathy and understanding.	Implement regular EQ development programs.	Ensure EQ training is not just an exercise but translates into daily practice.
Inclusive Mindset	Widening the leadership perspective to include diverse viewpoints.	Encourages innovation and a sense of belonging among employees.	Promote diversity in team compositions and decision-making processes.	Inclusivity efforts must go beyond token gestures to effect real change.
Cultural Dexterity	Maneuvering through diverse cultural landscapes with agility	Enables global and local market relevance and resonance.	Encourage continuous learning about diverse cultures and markets.	Avoid the pitfall of viewing cultural dexterity as a one-size-fits-all skill.

Section 7: Bringing It All Together: A Prelude to Inclusive Teams

The Reflective Journey: Embracing Inner Diversity

The foundational work of DEI mastery begins with the leader's internal exploration and acceptance of their multifarious inner landscape. We've underscored the crucial role of self-awareness as the bedrock upon which inclusive leadership is built. A self-aware leader is equipped to perceive and understand the rich complexity of their inner workings—acknowledging their biases, emotional triggers, and the lenses through which they view their team and the world at large.

This introspective process is not just about understanding oneself but also about how this self-knowledge translates into actions and decisions that shape the collective experience of the workforce. By embracing their internal diversity, leaders become a living example of the DEI principles they aim to instill in their organizations.

The Unseen Self: Illuminating Biases

We delved into the subtle yet profound impact of unrecognized biases on leadership efficacy. By bringing these biases into the light through self-assessment and training, leaders begin to dismantle the barriers to objective decision-making and fair management practices. This critical step prevents the percolation of prejudice into the organization's culture and ensures a level playing field for all team members.

Emotional Mastery: The Heart of Leadership

The discussion on emotional intelligence revealed its pivotal role in the human-centric approach to leadership. By cultivating emotional acuity, leaders harness the power to create a workplace that's not only productive but also supportive and empathetic. This emotional mastery is what enables leaders to connect with their teams on a deeper level, enabling trust and mutual respect.

Cultural Agility: Leading in a World of Difference

We emphasized the importance of cultural adaptability as a leadership skill in our interconnected world. By learning to navigate and accept the diversity of thoughts, beliefs, and practices, leaders prepare themselves and their organizations for global engagement and local sensitivity, turning diversity into a strategic advantage.

Forward to Inclusive Synergy: The Next Chapter

As we transition from personal transformation to team evolution, the next chapter promises to build upon these unique enhancements. Leaders will be guided on how to extend the principles of DEI from a self-centric practice to a group-centric triumph. We'll explore how to knit the threads of unique differences into a strong fabric of collective success, where each team member is an integral and valued part of the whole.

The upcoming chapter, "Fostering an Inclusive Team," will offer practical tools and strategies for building teams that respect diversity and leverage it for creativity, innovation, and performance. We will showcase how a leader's personal journey into self-awareness, bias recognition, emotional intelligence, and cultural adaptability is the precursor to creating teams that epitomize the essence of inclusion and equity.

Mastering Inclusive Leadership

In doing so, we will discuss team-building methodologies and illustrate how these approaches have been successfully implemented in various organizational contexts. We'll provide actionable steps for leaders to take, transforming their enhanced self-awareness into strategic team development—turning the distinct sparks of diversity into a flame of innovation and progress.

Looking Inward, Leading Outward

Self-Awareness	Recognizing Biases	Emotional Intelligence	Cultural Adaptability	Inclusive Leadership
The internal lens through which leaders view themselves and their actions	Unconscious inclinations that can shape workplace fairness and diversity.	The ability to understand and manage emotions in oneself and in others	The skill to navigate and recognize the complexities of a diverse workforce	The culmination of personal growth and skill development in maintaining an inclusive environment

The Collective Canvas: Painting a Team of Many Colors

Cultivating a Garden of Diversity

In the upcoming narrative, we delve into the art and science of creating a team as a mosaic of unique pieces to an intricate puzzle. We will examine how the richness of varied backgrounds, experiences, and perspectives can lead to innovative solutions and a more robust, resilient organization. This exploration will reveal the importance of each team member's contribution to the vitality and growth of the collective, much like diverse flora contributes to the ecosystem's health.

Leaders will be presented with strategies to encourage a workplace culture that doesn't just tolerate differences but actively seeks them out, recognizes them, and positions them as a driving force for creativity and innovation. This culture develops an environment where everyone feels safe to express their views, ask questions, and challenge the status quo, all within a framework that supports growth and learning.

Inclusion as the Soil for Growth

The focus will then shift to creating fertile ground where inclusion serves as the soil for personal and professional growth. We will guide leaders through the process of sowing seeds of trust and harvesting the fruits of collective

Enhancing Self-Perception

success. Readers will learn how to facilitate equitable participation, ensuring that all team members have equal opportunities to contribute and lead, regardless of their background or position within the company.

Leaders will gain insights into the complexities of power dynamics and learn how to balance them to nurture a sense of belonging and commitment. By cultivating an inclusive environment, they will enable their teams to not only accept but also celebrate the unique attributes each member brings to the table.

Strength in Weaving Together Distinct Threads

As leaders create a sense of community within their teams, the book will provide actionable steps to weave together the distinct threads of separate identities into a cohesive unit. The subsequent chapter will outline how to turn the concept of #**WeNotMe** into a living, breathing reality within teams. It will emphasize the collective over the individual, not to diminish personal achievement but to elevate the group's success as the ultimate goal.

We will explore practical methods for integrating diverse viewpoints into a unified vision, creating a chorus of voices that can speak as powerfully in harmony as they can in their solos. The process of achieving this balance is both delicate and deliberate, requiring a nuanced understanding of when to lead and when to listen.

Conclusion

The conclusion of this chapter and the segue into the next will encapsulate the transformation from a compliance-based approach to one that promotes a true sense of community. "From Compliance to Community"™ is more than a tagline; it represents the core ethos of the transformational leadership journey. It speaks to the shift from checking boxes to breaking down walls, from fulfilling obligations to fulfilling potential.

The narrative will underscore that the true spirit of DEI is not in the adherence to rules but in the embrace of shared humanity and the genuine desire to build a workplace where everyone feels they belong and can thrive. The next chapter will offer a blueprint for leaders to construct such a community, one where collective wisdom and the power of "we" steer the organizational ship towards uncharted but promising horizons. #**WeNotMe**

Mastering Inclusive Leadership

Chapter 2 Takeaways
Leading with Clarity and Inclusion

Key Area	Insights and Summaries	Actionable Steps for Leaders
Reflective Leadership	Introspect leaders can transform their interactions and team dynamics by aligning actions with awareness.	Engage in regular reflection, solicit feedback, and pursue coaching.
Bias Awareness	Recognizing the subtle influences of bias is essential for equitable decision-making and fair leadership.	Utilize self-assessment tools and undergo bias-awareness training to ensure balanced leadership.
Emotional Intelligence	Emotional acuity is a critical facet of leadership, influencing team harmony and effective conflict resolution.	Enhance emotional literacy through dedicated practices like active listening and emotional self-regulation.
Cultural Harmony	Leaders who adeptly navigate diverse cultures create synergistic and collaborative team environments.	Immerse in cross-cultural experiences and training to become champions of adaptability.
DEI Action Plan	A proactive approach to inclusivity uses self-awareness as a basis for building a culture of empowerment.	Foster a collective-centric leadership style, incorporating DEI principles into daily practices.
Integration and Anticipation	Summarizing the growth in self-awareness, bias management, emotional intelligence, and adaptability prepares for future team development.	Prepare to apply personal insights to cultivating an inclusive team dynamic in subsequent phases.
Diversity as Strength	Elevating diversity and enabling equitable participation fortify the team's vibrancy, fulfilling the #WeNotMe ethos.	Advocate for diversity as a cornerstone of team strength and enact policies that support this vision.

References

1. BetterUp. (n.d.). What is self-awareness and why is it important? Retrieved from - https://www.betterup.com/blog/what-is-self-awareness
2. BetterUp. (n.d.). Self-awareness in leadership. Retrieved from - https://www.betterup.com/blog/self-awareness-in-leadership
3. Business News Daily. (2017, January 4). Self-awareness in leadership. Retrieved from - https://www.businessnewsdaily.com/6097-self-awareness-in-leadership.html
4. Cleveland Clinic. (n.d.). Cognitive bias: How your mind plays tricks on you and how to avoid falling into its trap. Retrieved from - https://health.clevelandclinic.org/cognitive-bias/
5. CPD Online. (n.d.). Types of bias. Retrieved from - https://cpdonline.co.uk/knowledge-base/safeguarding/types-of-bias/
6. Ellevsen, G. (n.d.). Tips for achieving cultural adaptability. Retrieved from - https://www.linkedin.com/pulse/tips-achieving-cultural-adaptability-greg-ellevsen
7. Engagement Multiplier. (n.d.). How to create cultural adaptability in your company. Retrieved from - https://www.engagementmultiplier.com/resources/create-cultural-adaptability-in-your-company/
8. Forbes Coaches Council. (2018, February 15). Self-awareness: Being more of what makes you great. Forbes. Retrieved from - https://www.forbes.com/sites/ellevate/2018/02/15/self-awareness-being-more-of-what-makes-you-great/?sh=3c63e3be40dd
9. Forbes Business Council. (2021, June 23). Here's how to build a culture of adaptability. Forbes. Retrieved from - https://www.forbes.com/sites/forbesbusinesscouncil/2021/06/23/heres-how-to-build-a-culture-of-adaptability/?sh=235e5dd13b78

10. FranklinCovey. (2021). Unconscious bias self-assessment. Retrieved from - https://www.franklincovey.com/wp-content/uploads/2021/03/FranklinCovey-Unconscious-Bias-Self-Assessment.pdf
11. Get Impactly. (n.d.). Examples of personal biases. Retrieved from https://www.getimpactly.com/post/examples-of-personal-biases
12. Get Impactly. (n.d.). Bias awareness training. Retrieved from - https://www.getimpactly.com/post/bias-awareness-training
13. Harvard Business School Online. (n.d.). Emotional intelligence skills. Retrieved from - https://online.hbs.edu/blog/post/emotional-intelligence-skills
14. Harvard Division of Continuing Education Professional Development. (n.d.). How to improve your emotional intelligence. Retrieved from https://professional.dce.harvard.edu/blog/how-to-improve-your-emotional-intelligence/
15. HelpGuide. (n.d.). Emotional intelligence (EQ). Retrieved from https://www.helpguide.org/articles/mental-health/emotional-intelligence-eq.htm
16. IGI Global. (n.d.). Of chalk and chai. Retrieved from - https://www.igi-global.com/dictionary/of-chalk-and-chai/54050
17. Indeed Editorial Team. (n.d.). How to improve emotional intelligence. Indeed. Retrieved from - https://www.indeed.com/career-advice/career-development/how-to-improve-emotional-intelligence
18. Learning for Justice. (n.d.). Test yourself for hidden bias. Retrieved from - https://www.learningforjustice.org/professional-development/test-yourself-for-hidden-bias
19. Pagely. (n.d.). Emotionally intelligent CEOs. Retrieved from - https://pagely.com/blog/emotionally-intelligent-ceos/
20. Positive Psychology. (n.d.). Cognitive biases. Retrieved from - https://positivepsychology.com/cognitive-biases/
21. RocheMartin. (n.d.). 50 tips for improving your emotional intelligence. Retrieved from - https://www.rochemartin.com/blog/50-tips-improving-emotional-intelligence

22. The EW Group. (n.d.). How to adapt your communication across cultural differences. Retrieved from - https://theewgroup.com/blog/adapt-communication-cultural-differences/
23. Verywell Mind. (n.d.). What is self-awareness? Retrieved from https://www.verywellmind.com/what-is-self-awareness-2795023
24. Verywell Mind. (n.d.). Cognitive biases that distort your thinking. Retrieved from - https://www.verywellmind.com/cognitive-biases-distort-thinking-2794763
25. Verywell Mind. (n.d.). What is a cognitive bias? Retrieved from https://www.verywellmind.com/what-is-a-cognitive-bias-2794963
26. Young Entrepreneur Council. (n.d.). 10 ways to increase your emotional intelligence. Retrieved from - https://www.inc.com/young-entrepreneur-council/10-ways-to-increase-your-emotional-intelligence.html

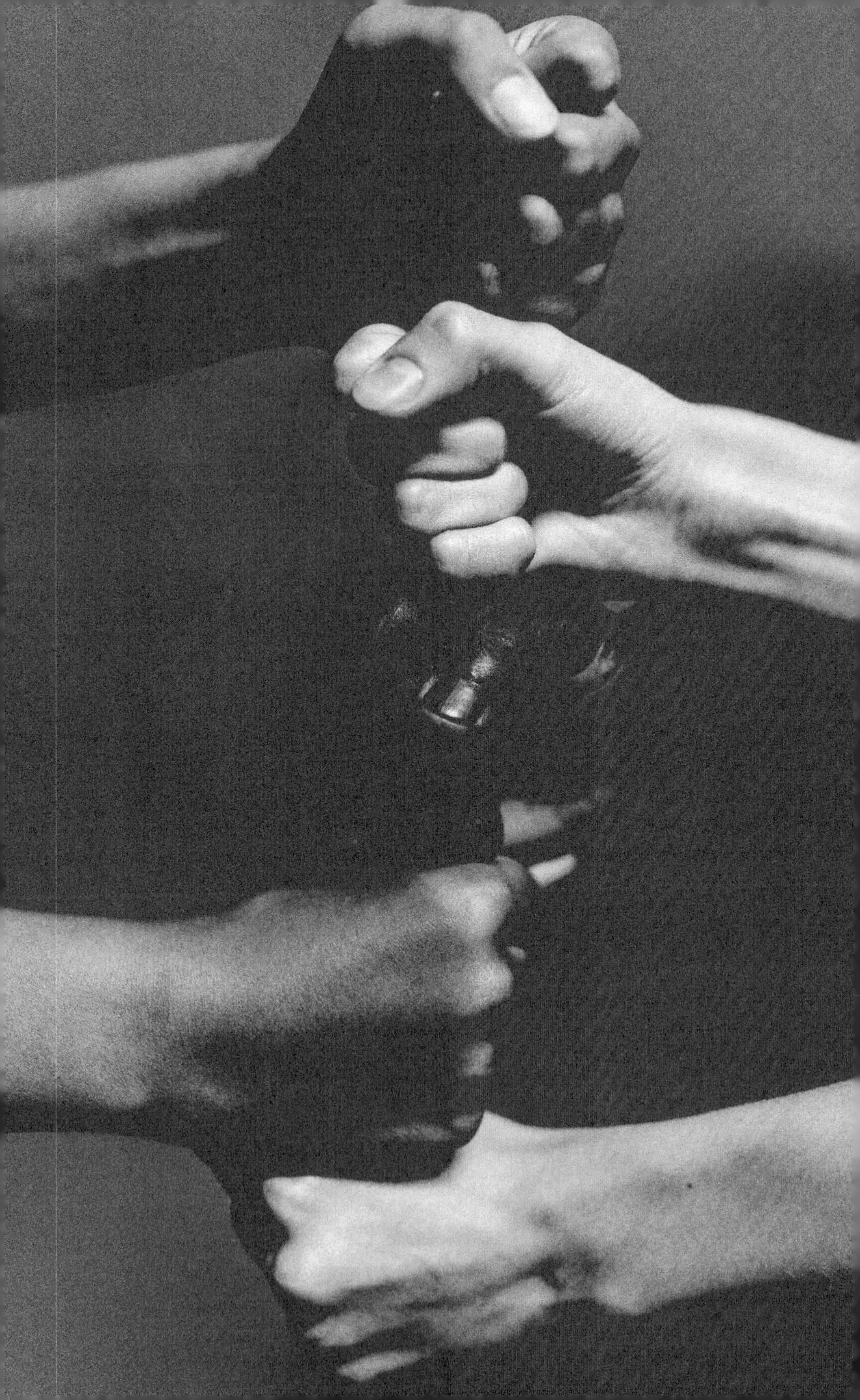

Chapter 3

Crafting Cohesion

"Teams thrive when every member feels they truly belong and their contributions matter."

- Marla Gottschalk, Industrial & Organizational Psychologist

The goal of this chapter is to explore the essence of crafting a team that not only embraces diversity but thrives on it. We explore the art of recruitment, the nuances of onboarding, and the subtleties of holding onto talent. As this chapter unfolds, you'll gain practical, actionable strategies designed to weave a fabric of diversity and cohesion within your organizational environment to move beyond Compliance (I/Me) to Community (Us/We).

Section 1: A Beacon of Inclusivity - Ernst & Young's (EY) Trailblazing Approach

EY: A Model for Corporate Success through DEI

EY stands as a testament to the power of DEI in shaping corporate success. This global leader in assurance, tax, transaction, and advisory services has embraced DEI not just as a compliance necessity but as a vital component of its organizational DNA. Their approach, deeply ingrained in authenticity and strategic foresight, offers a blueprint for how inclusivity can be a driving force in achieving organizational excellence (EY, 2021).

Integrating DEI into the Framework of Business Strategy

At EY, DEI is not a standalone initiative; it's interwoven into every aspect of their operations. From recruitment practices to leadership development, EY ensures that DEI principles are at the heart of their decision-making processes. This commitment is evident in their initiatives aimed at elevating women's prominence within the organization, transcending mere discourse, and leading to tangible outcomes in gender equity (Valor International, 2023).

EY's Framework: A Blend of Ethical Commitment and Strategic Execution

EY's DEI strategy stands on two pillars: ethical commitment and strategic execution. Their ethical commitment is rooted in the belief that a diverse and inclusive workforce is not just morally right but essential for encouraging innovation and understanding the global market. Strategically, EY implements DEI in a manner that aligns with their business goals, understanding that inclusivity directly contributes to their overall success.

Transformative Programs and Success Stories

Several programs have marked EY's progress in DEI. These initiatives range from mentorship channels designed to support underrepresented groups to tailored training programs that educate and sensitize their workforce on DEI issues. Such programs have not only enhanced the internal culture at EY but have also resonated externally, strengthening their brand as an inclusive and socially responsible organization.

The Impact of DEI on EY's Organizational Excellence

The impact of EY's DEI efforts is multifaceted. It's reflected in their ability to attract and retain top talent from diverse backgrounds, promoting an environment where different perspectives are respected and leveraged for creative solutions. Moreover, their commitment to DEI has been a crucial factor in building trust with clients and stakeholders, who increasingly appreciate social responsibility in their business partners.

EY's DEI Approach as a Guiding Light

EY's comprehensive approach to DEI serves as a guiding light for organizations aspiring to integrate inclusivity into their corporate ethos. By demonstrating that DEI can be both an ethical imperative and a strategic business advantage, EY offers valuable insights into how organizations can convert their DEI commitments into concrete, impactful actions.

Section 2: Strategies for Inclusive Recruitment, Onboarding, and Retention

The Genesis of Diversity: Inclusive Recruitment

In the space of inclusive team building, the initial foray begins with recruitment. EY exemplifies a model approach, constructing their recruitment process as a sturdy foundation for organizational diversity. Their strategies are meticulously designed to welcome diversity right from the outset, aligning with the insights of Hireology (2023) on the significance of inclusive recruitment.

A critical element in EY's strategy is the development of job descriptions. These are not mere lists of qualifications and duties; instead, they are carefully crafted to resonate with a broad audience. By using language that is inclusive and devoid of unconscious biases, EY ensures that the job descriptions appeal to a diverse pool of candidates. This approach aligns with Evalground's (2023) advocacy for job descriptions that are welcoming to all potential applicants, regardless of their background.

Beyond the written word, EY places considerable emphasis on the composition of their interview panels. These panels are meticulously assembled to mirror the diversity that the organization aspires to nurture. By doing so, EY not only cultivates a sense of belonging among diverse candidates but also enriches the interview process with varied perspectives. This practice resonates with Harver's (2023) findings, which highlight the importance of diverse interview panels in creating an equitable recruitment process.

EY's approach extends to the very channels through which they reach out to potential candidates. They engage in targeted outreach to various communities and networks, ensuring that their recruitment efforts are not confined to traditional pools of talent. This strategy not only widens the net of potential candidates but also demonstrates EY's commitment to bringing diverse voices into the fold.

EY's recruitment process is a testament to their dedication to diversity and inclusivity. From the initial job description to the final interview, every step is imbued with a commitment to welcoming a wide array of talents and backgrounds. This foundational approach sets the stage for a workforce that is not only diverse but also harmoniously integrated, reflecting the core principles of the organization.

Tailoring Onboarding for Universal Welcome

When new hires step into the world of EY, they encounter an onboarding experience that is not just about acclimatizing to a new role but about being embraced into a diverse family (Asana Wavelength, 2023). Drawing upon case studies from the Harvard Faculty of Arts and Sciences (2023) and Orion Talent (2023), we explore the nuances of creating an onboarding experience that serves as a model of inclusivity, setting the tone for an equitable and supportive work environment.

The Collective Canvas: Painting a Team of Many Colors

A Mosaic of Minds: Inclusive Recruitment

Recruitment is the canvas where the masterpiece of a diverse team begins. At EY, this process is not just about filling positions but about crafting a collection of minds and experiences. Inclusive recruitment at EY is a deliberate strategy to attract a spectrum of talent, ensuring that the diversity of the workforce mirrors the diversity of the world outside (Inclusive Employers, 2023).

The Gateway to Growth: Inclusive Onboarding

The initial days in a new organization are critical in shaping an employee's experience and perception. EY's onboarding process is a fine blend of welcoming new members into the fold and instilling in them the standards of inclusivity and equity (Aquent, 2023).

Cultivating Commitment: Strategies for Talent Retention

Employee retention is the art of maintaining a vibrant and committed workforce. At EY, this is achieved through a combination of ongoing development opportunities and an inclusive work environment (HubSpot, 2023).

Traversing the Terrain of Talent Preservation

Dimension	Blueprints from EY	Effective Tactics for Workforce Sustenance
Grasping Turnover Implications	EY's recognition of attrition costs	• Execute analyses comparing retention costs and turnover losses (PeopleKeep, n.d.) • Create a culture of growth and personal development (Enrich, n.d.)
Cultivating Lifelong Learners	Prioritizing continuous education	• Offer a spectrum of learning experiences that cater to different skill sets and interests (Continu, n.d.) • Integrate learning pathways with career growth prospects (Maryville University, n.d.)
Strategies for Longevity	Inclusivity at the core of development	• Establish mentorship opportunities that celebrate diversity (MentorcliQ, n.d.) • Design programs that address the unique aspirations and backgrounds of each team member (HBR, 2018)
Engagement and Empowerment	Active investment in employee engagement	• Implement training that enhances job satisfaction and involvement (eFront Learning, n.d.) • Encourage participation in decision-making and innovation (Thomas International, n.d.)
Nurturing a Vibrant Work Culture	Embracing DEI in all aspects of operations	• Initiate activities that foster a sense of belonging and appreciation for diversity (Bloomfire, n.d.) • Regularly assess and refine DEI strategies to stay aligned with evolving employee needs (HubSpot, n.d.)

Section 3: Building a Welcoming Team from Day One

The First Impression: Setting the Stage for Inclusion

Picture this: It's your first day at a new job. The air buzzes with anticipation, a blend of excitement and nervous energy. This moment, often underestimated, is pivotal in shaping your perception of your new workplace. First impressions, as fleeting as they are powerful, lay the groundwork for what's to come. In the realm of team building, the initial experience of a new member can significantly influence their sense of belonging and commitment.

Onboarding at EY is a harmonious blend of imparting essential job skills and embedding the company's ethos. As explored in various resources (EmployeeConnect, n.d.; Byars-Wright, n.d.; Encompass Insurance, n.d.; TrainingFolks, n.d.; Gallup, n.d.), effective onboarding programs integrate multiple dimensions:

Crafting an Effective Onboarding Experience

An impactful onboarding experience does far more than introduce a new hire to their role; it serves as a bridge connecting them to the very soul of the organization. EY stands as a testament to this approach, crafting an onboarding process that transcends basic job orientation and instills a deep sense of belonging and connection to the company's ideals and culture.

Introduction to Workplace Culture and Business Background

EY understands that a new employee's acclimation to the company's culture is as crucial as their role-specific training. Their onboarding program begins with an immersive introduction to EY's unique work environment, emphasizing their commitment to DEI (EmployeeConnect, n.d.). This introduction helps new hires grasp not just the day-to-day operations but also the underlying beliefs and ethos that drive EY.

Aligning with Business Mission, Objectives, and Ongoing Projects

The onboarding process at EY ensures that new team members understand the company's overarching mission and how their role contributes to it (ByarsWright, n.d.). This alignment is not just about understanding the

Crafting Cohesion

company's current projects but also about appreciating how these initiatives reflect EY's commitment to inclusivity and equity.

Connection with People: Building Relationships

EY places a high emphasis on interpersonal connections during onboarding. New employees are introduced to a network of colleagues and mentors who embody the company's diverse workforce (Gallup, n.d.). This step is pivotal in driving a sense of inclusion and support, making new hires feel like a part of the EY family from the beginning.

Familiarization with Workspace and Equipment

Ensuring comfort in the physical or digital workspace is another key aspect of EY's onboarding. This includes not only the practical elements of workspace and equipment but also an understanding of how these resources support a collaborative and inclusive work environment (Encompass Insurance, n.d.).

Overview of Internal Policies and Documents

Finally, EY's onboarding includes a thorough briefing on internal policies, especially those related to DEI. This step is crucial in setting expectations and standards for behavior and interactions within the company, reinforcing a culture of respect and inclusivity (TrainingFolks, n.d.).

Through these elements, EY's onboarding program effectively integrates new employees into the company's culture, mission, and community, ensuring that inclusivity is not just a policy but a lived experience from day one.

Integrating New Team Members: Creating a Tapestry of Inclusion

EY stands out for its exemplary integration of new team members, weaving them into the organizational fabric with a sense of belonging and recognition. This process is multi-faceted, addressing both professional and personal aspects of the workplace experience.

Weaving New Threads into the Team Fabric

Strategy	EY's Inclusive Approach	Benefits and Impact
First-Day Impressions	Personalized introductions emphasize the team's ethos (CPL, 2020).	Establishes an immediate sense of belonging and understanding of company objectives.

Building Social Bonds	Facilitating group activities for relationship-building (Forbes, 2017).	Enhances team cohesion and breaks down interpersonal barriers.
Guided Mentorship	Assigning experienced mentors for personalized support (Guider-ai, n.d.).	Accelerates adaptation and builds strong professional relationships.
Open Dialogue Culture	Encouraging transparent communication for feedback (Modern Aesthetics, 2017).	Promotes continuous improvement and addresses integration challenges promptly.
Inclusive Decision Involvement	Involving newcomers in decision-making processes (Legal Nature, n.d.).	Validates their contributions, supporting a sense of empowerment and inclusion.

Through these practices, EY exemplifies how to seamlessly integrate new team members, creating an environment where diversity is not just accepted but celebrated. The result is a vibrant, cohesive team where each member, regardless of their tenure, feels important and integral to the collective success.

Nurturing Inclusivity through Mentorship and Team Building

Beyond the formalities of onboarding lies the realm of informal yet crucial interactions. Mentorship programs and team-building exercises are the conduits through which inclusivity is nurtured and sustained. EY's approach to mentorship transcends traditional boundaries, nurturing connections that are both professionally enriching and personally empowering. Additionally, their team-building exercises are not mere formalities but platforms for genuine interaction and understanding across diverse backgrounds.

Section 4: Keeping Talent Through Ongoing Development

The Economics of Talent Retention: A Cost-Benefit Analysis

The balance between retaining and losing talent is a crucial financial consideration for any organization. The hidden costs of employee turnover often surpass the investments made in keeping staff. This reality is especially poignant in contexts where inclusivity and development are prioritized. Replacing an employee can be a costly affair, not just in terms of direct recruitment expenses but also through the loss of institutional knowledge, decreased morale, and the impact on team dynamics.

Crafting Cohesion

EY recognizes the significance of this economic balance. By emphasizing retention strategies that focus on inclusivity, EY mitigates these costs. According to PeopleKeep, the direct and indirect costs of replacing an employee can be substantial, including hiring, training, and the time it takes for a new employee to reach full productivity (PeopleKeep, n.d.). Enrich's research further highlights the ripple effects of turnover on financial wellness and organizational stability (Enrich, n.d.). By prioritizing retention through inclusivity, companies like EY are not only spurring a more diverse and cohesive environment but also ensuring economic efficiency and stability.

Engagement and Value through Continuous Learning

At the core of talent retention is the dual goal of keeping staff engaged and ensuring they feel valued. EY's commitment to continuous learning is a testament to this approach. Their focus on ongoing training and professional development is not merely a skill-enhancement strategy. It's a clear signal to employees about the organization's investment in their personal and professional growth.

This commitment is reflected in the diverse training opportunities provided, aligning with personalized career progression paths. As Continu (n.d.) notes, ongoing training is vital for employee engagement and retention. Maryville University (n.d.) also stresses the importance of aligning learning with career goals to enhance employee satisfaction and loyalty. Such initiatives contribute significantly to creating a workplace where each member feels they are an integral part of the organization's growth.

Ultimately, EY's approach to talent retention, focusing on inclusivity and continuous learning, serves as a blueprint for organizations aiming to balance economic efficiency with a commitment to employee development and engagement. This strategy not only enhances skills and knowledge but also builds a culture of inclusivity and belonging, crucial for long-term organizational success.

Mastering Inclusive Leadership

Section 5: Championing Retention Through Inclusive Practices

Retaining a Symphony of Voices

Talent retention, in the truest sense, is akin to conducting a symphony where every musician's contribution is vital. In the context of EY, their retention strategy transcends conventional norms, creating an orchestra where diversity of thought and background harmonizes to produce innovation and success (HBR, 2018). This illuminates EY's approach, illustrating how their practices in inclusivity and development have led to remarkable retention rates. MentorcliQ (2021) and Betterup (2022), confirm how inclusivity is intricately woven into the fabric of EY's retention strategies, creating a tapestry of engagement and belonging.

Mastering Talent Retention

Element	EY's Approach	Effective Practices
Understanding Costs	EY recognizes the significant financial implications of employee turnover. By quantifying these costs, they underscore the economic impact of retaining skilled staff.	• **Cost-Benefit Analysis:** Regularly assess the financial impact of retaining employees versus the costs involved in recruiting and training new staff (PeopleKeep, n.d.). • **Investment in Development:** Allocate resources towards comprehensive employee development programs, understanding that this investment leads to higher retention rates (Enrich, n.d.).
Continuous Learning	EY emphasizes continuous learning and development as key to employee engagement and retention. Their approach to ongoing training reflects a commitment to both personal and professional growth.	• **Diverse Training Opportunities:** Offer a wide array of training programs to cater to different learning styles and career paths (Continu, n.d.). • **Career Progression Alignment:** Ensure that training initiatives are closely aligned with customized career progression, developing advancement and growth (Maryville University, n.d.).

Crafting Cohesion

Retention Strategies	EY's retention strategies are deeply rooted in inclusivity. They focus on creating a work environment where everyone feels valued and supported, recognizing the diversity of their workforce.	• **Inclusive Mentorship Programs:** Develop mentorship initiatives that celebrate and support diversity, contributing to meaningful connections across different employee groups (MentorcliQ, n.d.). • **Tailored Development Initiatives:** Create and implement development programs that address the unique needs and aspirations of diverse employees, promoting a sense of belonging and inclusivity (HBR, 2018).

Elevating Teams Through Inclusion: Chapter Three Synopsis

This chapter highlights the vital role of DEI in corporate success, showcasing EY as a pioneer in integrating DEI into every aspect of their business strategy. This includes their commitment to ethical practices and strategic execution in developing a diverse workforce, crucial for innovation and global market understanding. EY's approach, characterized by mentorship schemes and tailored training programs, not only enhances their internal culture but also cements their reputation as an inclusive and socially responsible organization.

Having built an inclusive team, chapter four will explore how to maintain an environment where every member of the team feels safe to voice their opinions and contribute meaningfully. We'll investigate the importance of psychological safety and open communication in sustaining an inclusive culture, providing insights and strategies for nurturing a workplace where diversity is not just present but actively celebrated and leveraged for collective success as your organization shifts its mindset and practices from 'Compliance' to 'Community'. #**WeNotMe**

Navigating Team Diversity: Chapter Three Takeaways

Key Topics	EY's Approach & Insights	Impact & Implications
A Beacon of Inclusivity	EY sets a high bar in DEI, exemplifying how these principles drive corporate success.	Demonstrates the integral role of DEI in achieving organizational excellence.
Inclusive Recruitment	EY's recruitment is a cornerstone of their diversity strategy, ensuring a wide talent pool.	Highlights the importance of inclusive job descriptions and diverse interview panels in advancing diversity from the start.
Onboarding for Equity	Leveraging insights from Harvard Faculty of Arts and Sciences (2023) and Orion Talent (2023), EY's onboarding is designed to be inclusive.	Sets a welcoming tone for new employees, promoting an equitable and supportive work environment.
Strategic Talent Retention	EY's retention strategies focus on continuous learning and inclusivity, serving as a blueprint for a balance between economic efficiency and employee development.	Illustrates how inclusivity and development lead to effective talent retention.
Retention Strategies	EY's retention strategies are deeply rooted in inclusivity, emphasizing continuous learning and employee engagement.	Provides a model for how inclusivity can be woven into the fabric of organizational practices to retain diverse talent.

References

1. Bloomfire. (n.d.). Why ongoing training is important. Retrieved from-
   https://bloomfire.com/blog/buy-in-on-demand-ongoing-training/
2. Continu. (n.d.). The importance of ongoing training in the workplace. Retrieved from -
   https://www.continu.com/blog/ongoing-training
3. CPL. (2020). How to integrate new team members.
4. eFront Learning. (n.d.). Why managers should improve employee engagement through training. Retrieved from -
   https://www.efrontlearning.com/blog/2018/05/why-managers-improve-employee-engagement-training.html
5. Enrich. (n.d.). The true cost of employee turnover. Retrieved from -
   https://www.enrich.org/blog/The-true-cost-of-employee-turnover-financial-wellness-enrich
6. EvalGround. (n.d.). Inclusive hiring: Meaning and its importance. Retrieved from -
   https://evalground.com/blog/inclusive-hiring-meaning-and-its-importance/
7. Forbes. (2017). Seven ways to integrate new hires and make them feel welcome from the first day.
8. Guider-ai. (n.d.). Improve diversity and inclusion with mentoring.
9. Harvard Business Review. (2018). To retain employees, focus on inclusion — not just diversity. Retrieved from -
   https://hbr.org/2018/12/to-retain-employees-focus-on-inclusion-not-just-diversity
10. Hireology. (n.d.). The importance of inclusive recruitment. Retrieved from -
    https://hireology.com/blog/the-importance-of-inclusive-recruitment/

11. HubSpot. (n.d.). 3 strategies to increase employee retention. Retrieved from -

    https://blog.hubspot.com/marketing/3-strategies-to-increase-employee-retention

12. Legal Nature. (n.d.). Hiring employees: How to introduce and integrate new team members.

13. Maryville University. (n.d.). The importance of training and development in the workplace. Retrieved from -

    https://online.maryville.edu/blog/importance-of-training-and-development/

14. MentorcliQ. (n.d.). Improve DEI strategy for business. Retrieved from-

    https://www.mentorcliq.com/blog/improve-dei-strategy-for-business

15. Modern Aesthetics. (2017). 10 steps to integrate new employees.

16. Orion Talent. (n.d.). Inclusive onboarding. Retrieved from -

    https://www.oriontalent.com/recruiting-resources/blog/650/inclusive-onboarding

17. PeopleKeep. (n.d.). Employee retention: The real cost of losing an employee. Retrieved from -

    https://www.peoplekeep.com/blog/employee-retention-the-real-cost-of-losing-an-employee

18. Skillwork. (n.d.). The cost of hiring a new employee versus retaining one. Retrieved from -

    https://resources.skillwork.com/cost-of-hiring-new-employee-vs-retaining

19. Thomas International. (n.d.). Driving employee engagement through training and development. Retrieved from -

    https://www.thomas.co/resources/type/hr-blog/driving-employee-engagement-through-training-and-development

Crafting Cohesion

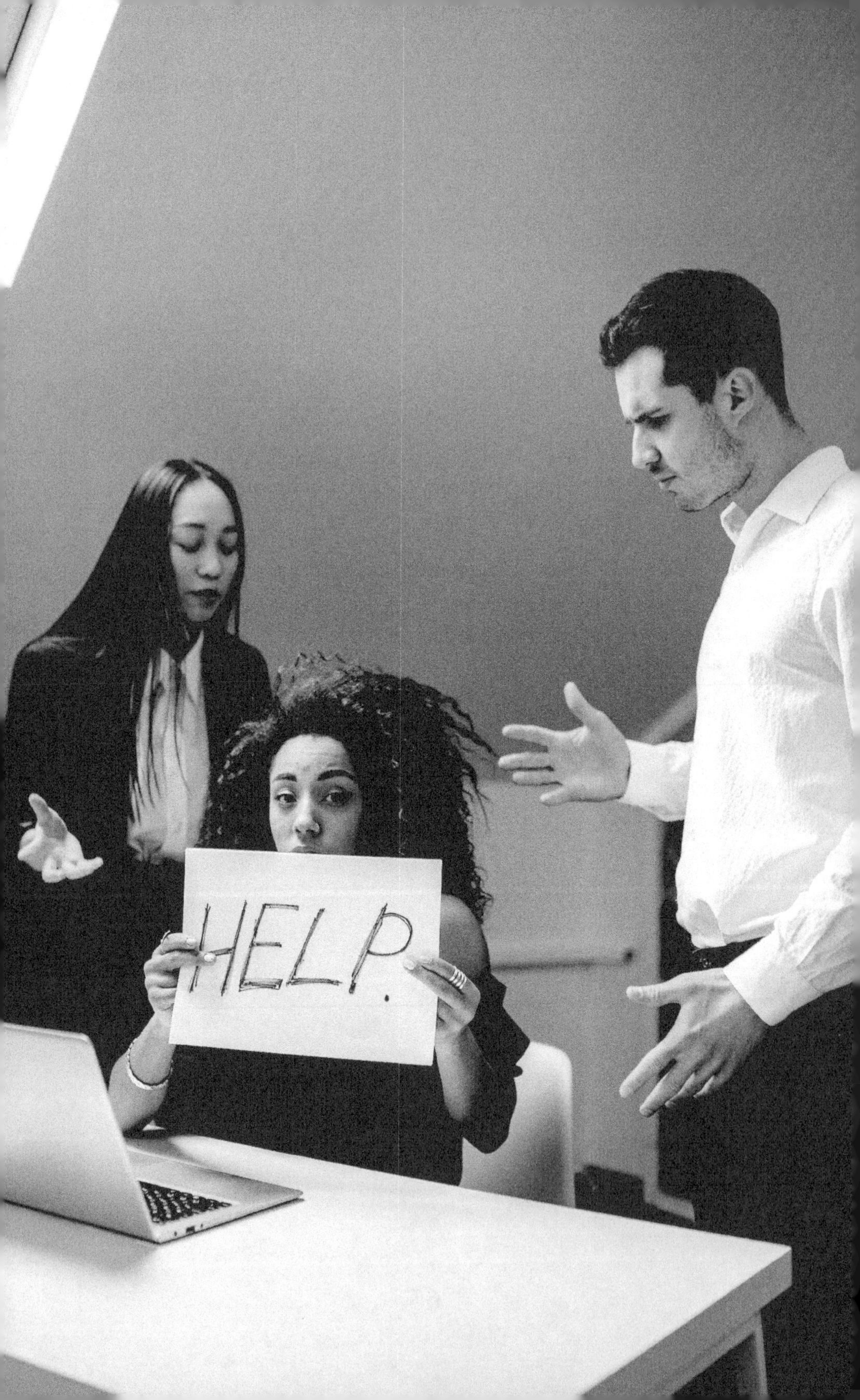
HELP.

Chapter 4

Validating Safe Spaces

"The human mind must believe in something, so it does well to watch its belief lest it be seized by something prejudiced or unscrupulous."

– Helen Keller

Section 1: Empowering Safe and Open Work Environments

In today's dynamic corporate environment, the creation of psychologically safe workspaces is essential. This chapter provides practical insights into crafting an environment where every team member feels confident and secure in voicing their opinions and ideas. Understanding and nurturing psychological safety can lead to significant improvements in team dynamics, creativity, and overall productivity.

Some contend that emphasizing psychological safety can lead to a culture of over-caution, where employees avoid healthy debates or challenging discussions for fear of causing offense. This could potentially stifle creativity and honest feedback, leading to "groupthink" and a lack of diverse perspectives. While it's true that a misinterpretation of psychological safety could lead to the avoidance of conflict if properly implemented, it actually encourages diverse viewpoints and constructive debates. A psychologically safe environment doesn't mean avoiding conflict but rather ensuring that disagreements are respectful and productive, leading to richer, more creative solutions.

Mastering Inclusive Leadership

As we progress through this chapter, you will learn techniques for nurturing a work culture that values open dialogue and respects diverse viewpoints. The aim is to equip you with the knowledge and tools needed to construct a work environment where psychological safety is a priority. This includes strategies for encouraging honest communication, recognizing and valuing the contributions of all team members, and establishing policies that ensure fairness and inclusivity.

Other opponents suggest that a heavy focus on open dialogue might lead to endless discussions with no concrete decisions or actions. They worry that this could hinder quick decision-making and efficient workflow. Open dialogue is not about prolonging discussions but about ensuring all relevant perspectives are considered. When team members feel heard and respected, decision-making becomes more informed and holistic, ultimately benefiting the organization's efficiency and effectiveness.

By providing examples and expert advice, these insights will help you implement strategies that create an environment where employees feel at ease taking risks, asking questions, and sharing their ideas without the fear of being mocked or facing consequences. This approach will enable you to transform your workplace into a space that actively encourages innovation and collaboration. Get ready to discover how to cultivate a work environment that not only embraces perspectives but also prioritizes the well being and engagement of every team member.

However, it's important to balance this focus on comfort and security with accountability and maintaining performance. Employees might feel too relaxed, leading to complacency. Psychological safety is about balancing comfort with accountability. It creates a space where employees are motivated to take risks and innovate because they know their ideas are valued and they won't be unfairly penalized for mistakes. This balance can actually drive higher performance and engagement.

Harmonizing Diversity: Booz Allen Hamilton's Pioneering DEI Framework

Those who are skeptical of heavy DEI investment feel that it might lead to a form of reverse discrimination, where decisions are made based on diversity quotas rather than merit, potentially compromising the quality of work and

Validating Safe Spaces

talent. Booz Allen Hamilton's (BAH) approach demonstrates that DEI, when implemented strategically, enhances meritocracy by leveling the playing field and allowing talent from diverse backgrounds to shine.

This approach doesn't lower standards but rather broadens the talent pool, leading to higher quality work and a more innovative environment. BAH's strategic embrace of DEI not only aligns with moral imperatives but also elevates their competitive edge. BAH's DEI strategy transcends superficial measures, embedding inclusivity into the core of their operations. This strategic integration has reaped benefits in creativity, employee engagement, and market relevance, setting a benchmark for corporate DEI practices (Forbes, 2023; LinkedIn, 2023).

Booz Allen Hamilton's DEI Leadership

(Note to Formatter – I tried to create a table and this needs reformatting)

Facet of DEI Success	Booz Allen Hamilton's Strategic Approach	Key Outcomes and Strategic Insights
Strategic Integration	DEI is seamlessly interwoven into all aspects of operations, signifying a holistic approach.	Leads to a workplace culture that values diversity at its core, setting industry benchmarks (Forbes, 2023; LinkedIn, 2023).
Innovation Catalyst	Leveraging DEI to promote an environment conducive to innovative thinking and diverse perspectives	Enhanced creativity and employee engagement are crucial for remaining competitive (LinkedIn, 2023).
Benchmark Setting	Established exemplary standards in corporate DEI, influencing industry-wide practices.	Recognition as a leader in DEI inspires other organizations to follow suit (Forbes, 2023).

Section 2: The Essence of Psychological Safety in the Workplace

The Domino Effect of Dismissed Voices

Consider a scenario where a team member, brimming with innovative thoughts, encounters a dismissive response during a meeting. Their idea, which is potentially transformational, is cast aside, leaving them feeling marginalized and undervalued. This not only stifles the person's future contributions but also robs the team of diverse perspectives. Such experiences underscore the critical need for psychological safety—an environment where every voice is heard and valued, encouraging a culture of mutual respect and innovation.

Objectors might fear that constantly catering to every team member's voice can slow down processes and lead to indecision. They believe that in certain situations, swift decision-making should take precedence over lengthy discussions to maintain efficiency. While efficiency is crucial, dismissing voices can lead to a lack of diverse perspectives, which is crucial for innovative and comprehensive solutions. Involving diverse viewpoints does not necessarily slow down decision-making; rather, it ensures that decisions are well-rounded and consider all aspects, ultimately leading to more effective and sustainable outcomes [HBR, 2023; McKinsey, 2023].

Component	Critical Insights on Psychological Safety	Leadership Actions for Enhancement
Essence of Safety	• Creating an environment where risk-taking and vulnerability are encouraged without fear of reprisal	• Leaders must cultivate empathy and a culture of open-mindedness (McKinsey, 2023; HBR, 2023).
Vital for Innovation	• Psychological safety is a key ingredient for team creativity and problem-solving capabilities.	• Promote a team ethos that values diverse perspectives and ideas (CCL, 2023; BetterUp, 2023).

Defining and Cultivating Psychological Safety

Psychological safety is the foundation of performing teams, characterized by an atmosphere where workers feel free to express themselves without fear of being ridiculed or facing retaliation. In such an environment, creativity thrives, leading to improved problem-solving abilities and better decision-making processes. Leaders play a role in establishing this climate by demonstrating empathy, openness, and a willingness to learn from every team member. Techniques such as active listening, acknowledging one's own limitations, and building an environment of mutual respect are instrumental in building psychological safety (CCL, 2023; BetterUp, 2023).

Opponents can view the concept of psychological safety as an excuse for employees to avoid accountability or become overly sensitive to feedback. They worry that this might create an overly permissive atmosphere where underperformance is tolerated. Psychological safety is not about shielding employees from accountability or constructive criticism. Instead, it's about developing a culture where feedback is delivered and received in a constructive manner.

This work environment promotes a culture of learning and continuous improvement. Employees are receptive to feedback and willing to take ownership of their actions. Leaders who practice empathy and active listening while maintaining high performance standards demonstrate that psychological safety and accountability can coexist and enhance each other.

The Stages of Psychological Safety

1. **Inclusion Safety: Cultivating a Broad Culture of Acceptance**

    Inclusion safety stimulates a workplace where employees feel free to express their identities and ideas. This openness enriches the workplace with a wide variety of perspectives essential for innovation and problem-solving (Edmondson, 2023). Inclusion safety sets a foundation of respect and acceptance, vital for cohesive team dynamics (McKinsey & Company, 2023).

2. **Learner Safety: Nurturing Growth and Innovation**

    Creating a safe space for learning and exploration encourages continuous improvement and innovation. When employees are not penalized for mistakes, they are more likely to propose creative solutions and drive progress (Delphinium, 2023). This learning-centric approach is key to employee retention, as it values and invests in personal and professional growth (SHRM, 2023).

3. **Contributor Safety: Boosting Engagement and Productivity**

   Acknowledging contributions enhances employee engagement and satisfaction (Predictive Index, 2023). When workers see their efforts recognized, their motivation and commitment increase, leading to heightened productivity. This engagement is crucial for a thriving and efficient workplace.

4. **Challenger Safety: Paving the Way for Change and Improvement**

   Encouraging employees to challenge norms produces a dynamic workplace (HBR, 2023). This openness to critique helps organizations stay agile and continuously improve. Empowering employees in this way contributes to a sense of ownership and investment in the company's success (CCL, 2023).

Section 3: The Impact of Psychological Safety Stages on Workers and Workplaces

Creating a Harmonious and Productive Workplace

Implementing these stages of psychological safety creates a workplace that balances differences with collective goals (Edmondson, 2023; McKinsey & Company, 2023). By prioritizing psychological safety, organizations unlock their workforce's full potential, leading to sustainable growth and success (BetterUp, 2023). Doubters argue that focusing too much on psychological safety can lead to a culture of complacency, where challenging the status quo or taking risks is discouraged. They believe that constant reassurance might hinder the development of resilience and adaptability in employees.

On the contrary, psychological safety encourages risk-taking and challenging the status quo within a supportive environment. It encourages employees to step outside their comfort zones, knowing that their ideas and efforts are respected even if they don't always result in success. This atmosphere establishes resilience and adaptability as employees learn from both failures and achievements within a setting, which ultimately drives innovation and progress.

Validating Safe Spaces

Business leaders might view the emphasis on psychological safety as a distraction from the primary business objectives, such as profit maximization and market competitiveness. However, psychological safety is not a diversion but a strategic enhancer of business objectives. Workplaces with high psychological safety witness increased employee engagement, innovation, and productivity, directly contributing to the bottom line. Additionally, organizations that prioritize psychological safety tend to have lower turnover rates, saving costs associated with recruiting and training new employees. These aspects ultimately contribute to a company's market competitiveness and financial success (BetterUp, 2023; Great Place to Work, 2023). Embedding psychological safety into the workplace culture is not just beneficial but essential for organizations aiming for long-term success and sustainability.

Overall, the positive impact of psychological safety on workers and workplaces is profound. It enhances employee well-being and satisfaction and drives innovation, productivity, and organizational health. Embedding these principles into the workplace culture is essential for organizations striving for excellence and sustainability.

Stage of Safety	Description and Significance	Leadership Actions for Support
Inclusion Safety	Stimulates a sense of belonging where employees can be their authentic selves.	Encourage sharing of diverse experiences and backgrounds (McKinsey, 2023; CCL, 2023).
Learner Safety	Encourages continuous learning and growth without fear of negative consequences for mistakes.	Create opportunities for learning and constructive feedback (BetterUp, 2023; HBR, 2023).
Contributor Safety	Employees feel valued for their contributions and believe their work has a purpose.	Recognize and celebrate individual contributions (CCL, 2023; McKinsey, 2023).
Challenger Safety	Empowers employees to challenge norms and propose innovative solutions.	Promote an environment where questioning and innovation are encouraged (HBR, 2023; BetterUp, 2023).

Section 4: Building Psychological Safety at Work

Facilitating Open Communication: The Lifeline of Inclusivity

The Impact of Communication Dynamics

Open communication is the lifeline that sustains the vitality of a diverse and inclusive workplace. Its presence, or lack thereof, directly influences team morale and project outcomes. An environment where communication flows freely encourages a deeper understanding of varied perspectives, leading to a sense of belonging and respect among team members. Conversely, restricted communication channels can lead to misunderstandings, reduced engagement, and a fragmented team dynamic.

Critics contend that excessive emphasis on open communication could lead to an overflow of unfiltered opinions, potentially causing decision-making paralysis and inefficiency. They worry that too much focus on everyone's input could dilute the clarity and direction of projects.

While it's important to manage the flow of communication, the benefits of open dialogue far outweigh the risks of potential overcommunication. Open communication encourages diverse perspectives, which leads to more robust decision-making and innovative solutions. It also generates a culture of trust and respect, essential for a thriving workplace. Properly managed, open communication can streamline decision-making processes by ensuring that all relevant viewpoints are considered, leading to more informed and effective outcomes (Indeed, 2023; JoinBlink, 2023).

Strategies to Enhance Open Dialogue

Cultivating open communication requires intentional efforts and structured approaches. Regular team check-ins, transparent feedback mechanisms, and inclusive decision-making forums are vital tools in this endeavor. Such practices not only ensure that every voice is heard but also reinforce the value of each contribution, thereby nurturing a culture of trust. may (Real8Group, 2023; ExtensisHR, 2023).

Leaders may worry that encouraging open communication could lead to certain voices dominating the conversation, overshadowing quieter team members. Effective strategies for open communication involve creating spaces where all voices can be heard equally. This includes not only encouraging team members to share their thoughts but also actively facilitating quieter members' participation and ensuring that dominant voices don't monopolize the conversation. Through structured approaches like round-robin sharing or anonymous feedback channels, leaders can create a more balanced and inclusive communication landscape, enhancing team dynamics and collaboration.

Enhancing Open Communication

Communication Dynamics	Impact of Open Communication in Diverse Teams	Strategies for Enriching Dialogue
Morale and Team Cohesion	Open dialogue enhances team morale and cohesion, supporting a productive and positive atmosphere.	Regular team meetings and feedback sessions are needed to encourage sharing and listening (Indeed, 2023; JoinBlink, 2023).
Diversity and Inclusion	Essential for ensuring all voices are heard, respected, and valued in decision-making processes.	Creating safe spaces for dialogue that respect and value diverse viewpoints (Forbes, 2023; BusinessNewsDaily, 2023).

Section 5: Establishing Fairness Through Policy

Lessons from Policy Implementation

The narrative of fairness in the workplace is often told through the lens of policy implementation. Policies that embody fairness and inclusivity lay the groundwork for a psychologically safe environment. These policies, however, must be more than mere documentation; they need to be living, breathing elements of the organizational ethos, consistently applied and adapted to meet evolving needs (Insights AMS, 2023).

Certain folks think that placing emphasis on policies could create a rigid and bureaucratic work environment, stifling creativity and spontaneity. They express concerns that strict adherence to policies might limit flexibility, hindering the organization's ability to adapt to situations or specific needs. While it is important to avoid rigidity, well-crafted policies play an essential role in ensuring fairness and consistency across the organization. Policies provide a clear framework for decision-making and behavior, promoting equity and preventing arbitrary actions. Flexibility can be built into policies by including provisions for exceptions or regular reviews to adapt to changing circumstances. This balanced approach ensures that policies serve their intended purpose without becoming constrictive.

Crafting and Enforcing Equitable Policies

Developing policies requires an understanding of the diverse needs and experiences of the workforce. These policies should be clear, fair, and aligned with the organization's core values. Additionally, effectively enforcing these policies is crucial to demonstrating the organization's commitment to fairness. Training programs that elucidate these policies enhance understanding and adherence, leading to a culture of integrity and respect (Small Business Chron, 2023; Indeed, 2023).

Some do worry that an intense focus on policy enforcement could lead to a culture of surveillance and distrust, where employees feel constantly monitored and judged against stringent standards. The key to effective policy enforcement lies in its approach. Instead of adopting a surveillance-focused approach, organizations should prioritize education, awareness, and support.

Enforcing policies in a transparent and constructive manner is essential for creating a respectful work environment. Training programs play a role in helping employees understand the reasons behind these policies and how they contribute to developing a positive workplace culture. This approach promotes a sense of ownership and commitment to policies, rather than a feeling of being policed.

Fairness Through Policy

Policy Focus	Significance and Implementation of Fair Policies	Guidelines for Policy Effectiveness
Creating a Safe Space	Policies are the bedrock for psychological safety, setting clear expectations and norms.	Develop clear, equitable policies that reflect organizational values and ethics (HBR, 2023; Insights AMS, 2023).
Fairness in Practice	Fair and inclusive policies are crucial for employee trust and organizational integrity.	Training and workshops to ensure comprehensive understanding and uniform enforcement (EmploySure, 2023; Small Business Chron, 2023)

Chapter 4 Conclusion and Transition: Exploring Contrasts and Confirmations

Section 6: The Interplay of Psychological Safety, Communication, and Policy: Acknowledging Challenges

As organizations embrace the principles of psychological safety, open communication, and fairness through policy, they recognize their integral role in creating a nurturing and productive workspace. These elements are not standalone ideals but are interconnected, each reinforcing the other to build a resilient and inclusive organizational culture where leaders shift their minds and actions from **Compliance** (I/Me) to **Community** (Us/We) **#WeNotMe**.

Skeptics say that the simultaneous implementation of psychological safety, open communication, and comprehensive policies can be overwhelming for organizations, especially smaller ones with limited resources. They might contend that focusing on too many areas at once could dilute efforts and lead to half-hearted implementations that don't effectively address any of the core areas.

While it is true that putting these practices into practice requires time and money, the synergy that results from their interconnectedness increases their impact. Psychological safety sets up an environment where open communication can thrive, and fair policies provide the structural backbone to sustain these cultural shifts. By integrating these elements cohesively, organizations create a more robust and supportive environment. Even small steps towards each area can lead to significant improvements in workplace culture and employee satisfaction (Edmondson, 2023; McKinsey & Company, 2023).

From Compliance to Community: Embracing the #WeNotMe Approach

Many detractors believe that transitioning from a focus on complying with rules to cultivating a sense of community might weaken standards and decrease accountability as the emphasis switches from performance to collective well-being.

Mastering Inclusive Leadership

However, moving from a compliance-centered mindset to one that's community-oriented does not undermine the importance of accountability. Instead, it strengthens it by placing it within a framework of support and shared accomplishments. In an environment that values community, everyone is encouraged to contribute their efforts, not out of fear of non-compliance but driven by their sense of belonging and purpose. This shift leads to motivation, engagement, and productivity among employees, ultimately benefiting both employees and the organization as a whole (HBR, 2023; Great Place to Work, 2023).

While the path to building a workplace that prioritizes psychological safety, open communication, and fair policies may have its challenges, the benefits of such an environment are clear. It leads to a more dynamic, innovative, and cohesive workforce, ultimately driving organizational success. As we move into the next chapter, we'll explore how authentic leadership plays a pivotal role in reinforcing and sustaining these cultural shifts.

Looking ahead, Chapter 5 will examine the art of authentic leadership. We will explore how leaders can exemplify their true selves in an environment where authenticity is not only accepted but celebrated, thereby setting a precedent for their teams to follow.

References

1. Booz Allen Hamilton. (2023). Forbes Says Booz Allen Among Best for Diversity. Retrieved from -

   https://www.boozallen.com/menu/media-center/q1-2023/forbes-says-booz-allen-among-best-for-diversity.html

2. LinkedIn - Booz Allen Hamilton. (2023). Proud to be named No. 1. Retrieved from -

   https://www.linkedin.com/posts/booz-allen-hamilton_we-are-proud-to-have-been-named-no-1-on-activity-6833100548393308160-UWQZ

3. Edmondson, A. C. (2023). What is Psychological Safety. Harvard Business Review. Retrieved from -

   https://hbr.org/2023/02/what-is-psychological-safety

4. 4Center for Creative Leadership. (2023). What is Psychological Safety at Work? Retrieved from -

   https://www.ccl.org/articles/leading-effectively-articles/what-is-psychological-safety-at-work/

5. McKinsey & Company. (2023). What is Psychological Safety. Retrieved from -

   https://www.mckinsey.com/featured-insights/mckinsey-explainers/what-is-psychological-safety

6. BetterUp. (2023). Why Psychological Safety at Work Matters. Retrieved from -

   https://www.betterup.com/blog/why-psychological-safety-at-work-matters

7. Great Place to Work. (2023). Psychological Safety Workplace. Retrieved from -

   https://www.greatplacetowork.com/resources/blog/psychological-safety-workplace

8. Delphinium. (2023). 9 Ways Leaders Can Create Psychology Safety at Work. Retrieved from -

   https://delphiniumcc.co.uk/9-ways-leaders-can-create-psychology-safety-at-work/

9. SHRM. (2023). Leaders Build Psychological Safety for Teams. Retrieved from -

   https://www.shrm.org/executive/resources/articles/pages/leaders-build-psychological-safety-teams.aspx

10. Harvard Business Review. (2022). A Guide to Building Psychological Safety on Your Team. Retrieved from -

    https://hbr.org/2022/12/a-guide-to-building-psychological-safety-on-your-team

11. Predictive Index. (2023). Psychological Safety in the Workplace. Retrieved from -

    https://www.predictiveindex.com/blog/psychological-safety-in-the-workplace

12. Accelerate at University of Utah Health. (2023). Setting the Stage for Psychological Safety: 6 Steps for Leaders. Retrieved from -

    https://accelerate.uofuhealth.utah.edu/resilience/setting-the-stage-for-psychological-safety-6-steps-for-leaders

13. Indeed. (2023). What is Open Communication. Retrieved from -

    https://www.indeed.com/career-advice/career-development/what-is-open-communication

14. Blink. (2023). The Importance of Open Communication. Retrieved from -

    https://www.joinblink.com/intelligence/open-communication-importance

15. Forbes Tech Council. (2021). Communication is Key When Fostering an Open and Diverse Work Environment. Retrieved from -

    https://www.forbes.com/sites/forbestechcouncil/2021/04/26/communication-is-key-when-fostering-an-open-and-diverse-work-environment/?sh=24ef36785759

16. Business News Daily. (2023). Diversity Inclusive Communication. Retrieved from -

    https://www.businessnewsdaily.com/9488-diversity-inclusive-communication.html

17. Small Business - Chron. (2023). Communication Diversity Workplace. Retrieved from -

    https://smallbusiness.chron.com/communication-diversity-workplace-11389.html

18. Real8 Group. (2023). How to Maintain Open Communication in the Workplace. Retrieved from -

    https://www.real8group.com/how-to-maintain-open-communication-in-the-workplace/#

19. Inside.6Q. (2023). Open Communication in the Workplace. Retrieved from -

    https://inside.6q.io/open-communication-in-the-workplace/

20. ExtensisHR. (2023). 5 Ways to Foster an Open Communication Office Culture. Retrieved from -

    https://extensishr.com/resource/5-ways-to-foster-an-open-communication-office-culture/

21. Executive Leader. (2023). Effective Leaders Foster Open Communication. Retrieved from -

    https://executiveleader.com/effective-leaders-foster-open-communication/

22. Thoughtful Leader. (2023). Encouraging Open Communication. Retrieved from -

    https://www.thoughtfulleader.com/encouraging-open-communication/

23. Leaders.com. (2023). Open Communication. Retrieved from -

    https://leaders.com/articles/company-culture/open-communication/

24. We Are AMS. (2023). Business Case Versus The Fairness Case For Diversity. Retrieved from -

https://insights.weareams.com/post/102hqrh/business-case-versus-the-fairness-case-for-diversity

25. The Human Capital Hub. (2023). 11 Reasons Why Workplace Fairness Matters For Every Employer. Retrieved from -

    https://www.thehumancapitalhub.com/articles/11-Reasons-Why-Workplace-Fairness-Matters-For-Every-Employer

26. PerformHR. (2023). Why is Fairness Important in Workplace. Retrieved from -

    https://performhr.com.au/why-is-fairness-important-in-workplace/

27. Harvard Business Review. (2022). How Fair is Your Workplace. Retrieved from -

    https://hbr.org/2022/07/how-fair-is-your-workplace

28. Employsure. (2023). The Importance of Workplace Policies and Procedures. Retrieved from -

    https://employsure.com.au/blog/the-importance-of-workplace-policies-and-procedures/

29. Small Business - Chron. (2023). Enforce Policies Consistently Work. Retrieved from -

    https://smallbusiness.chron.com/enforce-policies-consistently-work-10970.html

30. Indeed. (2023). Fairness in the Workplace. Retrieved from -

    https://www.indeed.com/career-advice/career-development/fairness-in-the-workplace

31. Wolters Kluwer. (2023). Workplace Rules for Business Owners and Employees. Retrieved from -

    https://www.wolterskluwer.com/en/expert-insights/workplace-rules-for-business-owners-and-employees

32. The New York Times. (2023). Workplace Fairness. Retrieved from -

    https://archive.nytimes.com/www.nytimes.com/allbusiness/AB11382173_primary.html?pagewanted=print

Validating Safe Spaces

Mastering Inclusive Leadership

Chapter 5

Embodying Authentic Leadership

> "A leader takes people where they want to go. A great leader takes people where they don't necessarily want to go but ought to be."
>
> -Former First Lady Rosalynn Carter

Section 1: Building Genuine Leadership in Diverse Environments

Chapter 5 breaks down the intricacies of authentic leadership and sheds light on how it functions in inclusive and diverse work environments. This segment aims to demystify the concept of genuine leadership, emphasizing its pivotal role in creating an environment of inclusive decision-making and driving a culture grounded in integrity and respect.

This chapter showcases innovative corporations worldwide, including Slack, which is renowned for its progressive approach to DEI. These organizations, lauded for their comprehensive DEI strategies, exemplify the profound effects of embedding genuine leadership within their corporate culture. These effects manifest in heightened innovation, employee engagement, and a competitive edge in the market (Social Talent, 2023; Melyssa Barrett, 2023; Fast Company, 2023; Engagedly, 2023; CIO, 2023; TeamBuilding, 2023).

The goal is to deepen your understanding of genuine leadership. We explore its foundational elements, guiding leaders to weave authenticity seamlessly into their leadership practices. This isn't just about personal growth; it's about nurturing an organizational culture that cherishes a variety of opinions, upholds equity, and ensures widespread participation. Authentic leaders are pivotal in crafting such environments, modeling behavior through their decisions and actions, and cultivating a workspace where every individual's perspective is valued and every effort is acknowledged.

Furthermore, this segment offers tangible strategies and training methods to develop their authentic leadership capabilities. From enhancing self-awareness to practicing open and honest communication, leaders will uncover effective ways to adapt to the nuances of modern, wide-ranging workplace settings. The emphasis is placed on practical applications, offering actionable steps and training approaches for honing genuine leadership skills—essential for leaders striving to adopt an inclusive, vibrant, and innovative work environment.

This exploration is an invitation to current and future leaders poised to accept the challenge of leading with authenticity in a world where diversity is not just recognized but fervently celebrated. Prepare to explore the enriching potential of authentic leadership and its significant impact on cultivating inclusive and prosperous workplaces.

Nurturing Authentic Leadership for Organizational Advancement

Element	Explanation	Influence
Genuine Leadership	Leadership style rooted in honesty and ethical clarity that inspires and empowers others to reach their full potential.	Bolsters trust, stimulates innovation, and enhances team cohesion (Social Talent, 2023; Melyssa Barrett, 2023)
DEI Implementation	Examples from top companies with effective DEI strategies demonstrate the positive impact of an inclusive culture	Illustrates the positive outcomes of integrating genuine leadership within DEI frameworks (Fast Company, 2023; CIO, 2023)
Leadership Development	Focus on cultivating self-awareness and clear communication skills to contribute to a thriving work environment.	Equips leaders to align actions with core values, nurturing a trustworthy and inclusive environment (Engagedly, 2023; TeamBuilding, 2023)

Section 2: Innovative Integration of DEI in Corporate Culture: Understanding Slack's Approach to DEI

Slack's approach to diversity, equity, and inclusion (DEI) is not just a peripheral initiative; it is a core aspect of their business model. This tech giant has embraced DEI as an integral part of its operations, creating a workspace where diversity is not just accepted but celebrated. Their strategy exemplifies a unique blend of authentic leadership and proactive initiatives, setting a benchmark in corporate DEI practices. This is evident from their detailed reports and continuous efforts to improve diversity metrics within the company (Slack, 2019).

Slack's commitment to DEI is a testament to their innovative and forward-thinking approach in the tech world. Their leadership style, deeply rooted in authenticity and inclusivity, has become a beacon in corporate DEI practices. This commitment is not merely a policy; it's woven into Slack's organizational fabric, making inclusivity a natural aspect of their work culture.

The Counterpoint: DEI as a Superficial Facade

Some critics declare that corporate DEI initiatives are often superficial, serving more as a public relations tool than effecting real change. They contend that companies like Slack might emphasize diversity in their external communications while failing to address systemic issues internally. This view suggests that DEI efforts are more about brand image than a genuine commitment to change.

Debunking the Skepticism: Slack's Tangible DEI Achievements

However, Slack's approach debunks this skepticism through its tangible actions and transparent reporting. For instance, Slack's 2019 diversity report showcases their commitment to not only hiring unique talent but also nurturing an inclusive environment where every employee feels valued (Slack, 2019). Their efforts to improve diversity in leadership positions and their commitment to equitable pay practices are a testament to their genuine commitment to DEI. Furthermore, articles like the one in "The Atlantic" highlight how Slack's focus on diversity has given them a competitive edge in the tech industry, developing a culture of innovation and creativity (The Atlantic, 2018).

Implementing DEI Beyond Tokenism

At Slack, DEI is more than just meeting quotas or ticking boxes. It's about creating a work environment that mirrors the diverse world we live in. Their strategy involves not only recruiting a range of talent but also ensuring that these employees have equitable opportunities for growth and development. This approach counters the notion that DEI is merely for optics, proving that when implemented thoughtfully, it contributes significantly to the company's success both culturally and financially.

Inclusive Leadership as a Driving Force

A key factor in Slack's DEI success is their leadership's commitment to authenticity and inclusivity. By setting a tone at the top that values numerous perspectives, Slack's leadership ensures that DEI is a living, breathing part of the company culture. This leadership style has been crucial in creating a space where employees from all backgrounds feel they belong and can thrive.

Ultimately, Slack's DEI approach, deeply embedded in its organizational DNA, serves as an inspiring model for other corporations. It demonstrates that a true commitment to diversity, equity, and inclusion can lead to a more dynamic, innovative, and successful business.

Slack's DEI Framework

Aspect	Details of Slack's DEI Approach	Counterpoints and Rebuttals
Core Integration of DEI	Slack has seamlessly integrated DEI into its core operations, going beyond policy to embed it into its organizational DNA. This approach produces a workspace that celebrates diversity and inclusivity as the norm (Slack, 2019).	Some see DEI initiatives as mere PR tactics. However, Slack's tangible actions, such as equitable pay practices and leadership diversity, demonstrate a deep commitment (Slack, 2019).
DEI as a Business Model	DEI is treated as a vital aspect of business strategy, contributing to Slack's competitive edge in the tech industry. Their continuous improvement in diversity metrics highlights this commitment (The Atlantic, 2018).	Opponents believe DEI is often for brand image. Slack's transparent reporting and improvement efforts refute this, showing real internal systemic changes (The Atlantic, 2018).

Leadership and DEI	Slack's leadership plays a critical role in driving the DEI agenda. Their authentic, inclusive leadership style is essential to creating an environment where employees of all backgrounds feel valued (Slack, 2019).	While some leaders may not fully embrace DEI, Slack's leadership actively promotes it, ensuring DEI is integral to company culture (Slack, 2019).

Section 3: The Real You: Embracing Authentic Leadership

Embracing Vulnerability: A Paradigm Shift in Leadership

Picture a leader who chooses to embrace vulnerability and remove their mask of infallibility, consistently producing excellent results. This leader, once known for their rigid, authoritative approach, began to show aspects of their true self—uncertainties, thoughts, and genuine emotions. This act of courage transformed the team's dynamic, replacing fear and silence with trust and open communication. The team started to express their ideas more freely as a result of their leader's honesty, breeding a culture of creativity and innovation.

The Essence of Authentic Leadership

Authentic leadership revolves around being genuine in interactions and transparent in actions. It involves aligning leadership style with personal values and ensuring decisions are made ethically and transparently. Ultimately, leaders who incorporate their personal ethos of empathy and collaboration into their leadership approach result in a more engaged and motivated team.

Core Components of Authentic Leadership

In the landscape of contemporary leadership, authenticity is not just a desirable trait but a crucial foundation for meaningful and influential guidance. Here are the pivotal components that constitute authentic leadership.

- **Self-Awareness:** Central to authentic leadership is the element of self-awareness. This enables leaders to recognize their strengths and acknowledge their limitations, while also managing their emotions effectively (Harappa Education, n.d.). It's a reflective journey that empowers leaders to be mindful of their impact on others.

- **Ethical Decision-Making:** The ethical underpinnings of authentic leadership are non-negotiable. It encompasses making choices that are effective and morally sound. (Indeed, n.d.). This ethical compass guides them away from unethical shortcuts, ensuring that their decisions are aligned with the highest standards of integrity and moral responsibility.

- **Transparency:** Trust is a fundamental aspect of leadership, and transparency is the pathway to building it. Authentic leaders are characterized by their openness regarding their intentions and decisions, creating an environment where trust and respect thrive (CCL, n.d.).

- **Consistency:** A key hallmark of authentic leadership is the alignment between words and actions. This consistency is vital in maintaining trust and reliability, assuring team members that their leader is steadfast in their commitment (HBS Online, n.d.). It creates a stable and predictable environment, conducive to both personal and professional growth within the team.

- **Genuine Interactions:** Engaging in genuine interactions is the final cornerstone of authentic leadership. This requires nurturing relationships that are caring, supportive, and sincere, demonstrating a leader's dedication to the well-being and professional development of their team (WGU, n.d.). It cultivates a workplace culture where every individual feels recognized, heard, and inspired to achieve their best.

Component	Description	Impact on Leadership
Self-Awareness	Understanding one's strengths, limitations, and emotions allows leaders to make more informed decisions and effectively manage their own behavior.	Enhances leaders' ability to recognize and adjust their impact for more effective leadership (Harappa Education, 2023).
Ethical Decision-Making	Prioritizing morality and integrity in decisions is essential for encouraging trust and maintaining a positive organizational culture.	Builds trust and respect by ensuring decisions align with core values and ethics (Indeed, 2023; CCL, 2023).

Transparency	Being open about intentions and decisions cultivates trust and promotes an environment of honesty and accountability.	Cultivates a culture of trust and open communication within the team (Harvard Business School, 2023; BetterUp, 2023).
Consistency	Maintaining alignment between words and actions is essential for building trust and credibility.	Encourages trust and reliability with actions that consistently mirror stated values (WGU, 2023; Forbes, 2023).
Genuine Interactions	Engaging in sincere interactions with concern for others builds authentic relationships and enhances mutual respect and understanding.	Strengthens team connections, leading to enhanced collaboration and understanding (Natural Talent, 2023; Skillcast, 2023).

Section 4: The Positive Butterfly Effect of Authentic Leadership

The Spark of Innovation and Change

The adoption of an authentic leadership style can initiate a lasting reverberation within an organization. When leaders adopt genuine and transparent approaches, it instills a culture of trust and openness. This was evident in the case of a leader who transitioned to a more authentic style, leading to a noticeable shift in team dynamics. Their new approach resonated throughout the team, cultivating an environment where innovative ideas flourished, and team members felt valued and empowered to share their thoughts.

This positive change not only enhanced the team's creativity and performance but also inspired other managers in the organization to adopt a more authentic and people-centric leadership style. The result was a widespread cultural shift towards more authentic leadership practices across the company, significantly improving the organization's overall performance and employee satisfaction (Harappa Education, 2023; Indeed, 2023).

Training for Authentic Leadership

Leaders who aspire to embody authenticity can significantly benefit from dedicated training programs. These programs focus on enhancing self-awareness, honing ethical reasoning skills, and promoting transparent communication. Through various methods, such as reflective practices,

Mastering Inclusive Leadership

navigating ethical dilemmas, and communication skill-building workshops, these training initiatives help leaders align their actions with their values and principles. Such training equips leaders with the tools and mindset necessary to lead authentically, supporting a culture of trust and integrity within their teams (Natural Talent, 2023; Skillcast, 2023).

Walk the Talk: Leading by Example

The principle of leading by example is fundamental to authentic leadership. When leaders consistently embody the values they advocate, it sets a powerful example for the team. This alignment between what leaders say and do not only builds trust but also shapes the organizational culture in a positive way. Particularly in various environments, leading by example is crucial, as it sets clear standards for behavior and judgment, promoting an inclusive and respectful work culture. By demonstrating integrity, consistency, and openness, leaders can effectively inspire their teams and establish a positive, value-driven work environment (BetterUp, 2023; Forbes, 2023).

Everyone's Voice Matters: Inclusive Decision-Making

Inclusive decision-making is a vital component of authentic leadership. A clear demonstration of this was when a leader involved every team member in decision-making, leading to the revival of a stalled project. This approach values diverse perspectives and leverages collective intelligence, resulting in innovative and well-rounded solutions. Techniques to develop inclusive decision-making include ensuring all voices are heard, creating mutual understanding, developing inclusive solutions, and generating shared responsibility. These practices not only enhance project outcomes but also contribute to a more engaged and committed team (HBS Online, 2023; Psychology Today, 2023).

Section 5: The Limitations of Authentic Leadership

Some skeptics argue that authentic leadership, while idealistic, may not always be practical or effective in all organizational contexts. They suggest that being overly transparent and vulnerable might undermine a leader's authority or decision-making power. Additionally, they worry that a leader's authentic self may not always align with the organization's needs or goals, leading to conflicts or inconsistencies in leadership.

Debunking the Skepticism: Effectiveness of Authentic Leadership in Diverse Contexts

Despite these concerns, evidence shows that authentic leadership is highly effective in establishing a positive organizational culture. For instance, the case of the healthcare leader demonstrates how authenticity can transform team dynamics and improve cohesion and effectiveness (CCL, 2023; Harvard Business School, 2023). Authentic leadership does not equate to oversharing or a lack of discretion; instead, it involves being true to one's values while also being adaptable and responsive to the organization's needs. This style of leadership promotes trust and respect, which are crucial for a productive work environment.

Training for Authentic Leadership: Addressing Concerns

While some may consider training for authentic leadership as unnecessary or abstract, the benefits are tangible. Training programs that focus on self-awareness and ethical decision-making equip leaders to navigate complex situations while staying true to their values (Natural Talent, 2023; Skillcast, 2023). These programs help leaders strike the right balance between being genuine and maintaining professional discretion, ensuring their leadership style is both authentic and effective.

Leading by Example: Overcoming Perceived Weaknesses

Detractors might perceive leading by example as potentially limiting, especially if a leader's personal style does not resonate with all team members. However, leading by example is about embodying core values like integrity and openness, which are universally respected and effective in diverse environments (BetterUp, 2023; Forbes, 2023). This approach does not confine leaders to a specific style but encourages them to be role models for ethical and inclusive behavior, which positively influences the entire team.

Inclusive Decision-Making: Beyond Slow Processes

A common criticism of inclusive decision-making is that it can slow down processes and lead to indecision. However, the example of the stalled project revival illustrates that inclusive decision-making can lead to more innovative and effective outcomes (HBS Online, 2023; Psychology Today, 2023). When diverse perspectives are considered, decisions are more comprehensive and well-rounded, ultimately benefiting the organization's success.

Mastering Inclusive Leadership

In conclusion, while authentic leadership may have perceived limitations, its practical application demonstrates significant benefits for organizational culture, team dynamics, and overall effectiveness. Leaders who genuinely embody these principles create a positive ripple effect, driving change and instilling an inclusive and innovative environment.

Chapter Five Conclusion: The Change-Making Power of Authentic Leadership

Authentic leadership, characterized by genuine action and inclusive management, transcends theoretical ideals. It manifests as tangible practices that can drastically alter an organization. Leaders who embrace and exemplify these principles catalyze change and promote a culture that is both inclusive and innovative. Such leadership not only drives organizational success but also cultivates an environment where every team member feels valued, respected, and empowered to contribute their best.

Chapter 5 Key Takeways: Embracing Authentic Leadership for Organizational Transformation

Aspect	Description	Impact
Authentic Leadership	Leading with vulnerability, honesty, and transparency fosters trust and encourages open communication within the organization.	Breeds trust, encourages innovation, and improves team dynamics (Harappa Education, 2023; Indeed, 2023)
Training for Authenticity	Focusing on self-awareness and ethical thinking to promote a culture of trust and integrity within the organization.	Equips leaders with skills for authentic leadership, promoting trust and integrity (Natural Talent, 2023; Skillcast, 2023)
Leading by Example	Aligning actions with advocated values and demonstrating ethical behavior in all aspects of their work.	Sets a standard for behavior, inspiring teams and shaping positive culture (BetterUp, 2023; Forbes, 2023)
Inclusive Decision-Making	Valuing diverse perspectives in decision processes and promoting collaboration among team members.	Leads to innovative solutions and a more engaged team (HBS Online, 2023; Psychology Today, 2023)

Chapter 6 Preview: Navigating Challenges in Diversity and Inclusion Efforts

As we investigate the nuances of authentic and inclusive leadership, it's important to recognize the potential challenges that may arise. Chapter 6 explores strategies for identifying and overcoming obstacles in diversity and inclusion initiatives, ensuring sustained progress and success in creating inclusive work environments. While embracing authenticity and inclusivity is key, leaders must also be prepared to face and navigate challenges on their journey toward achieving organizational excellence and shifting their mindset from **I/Me** to **We/Us** as they move from "**Compliance to Community.**"™ See you at the top. #**WeNotMe**

References

1. BetterUp. (n.d.). Authentic leadership. BetterUp. Retrieved from - https://www.betterup.com/blog/authentic-leadership
2. BetterUp. (n.d.). Leading by example. BetterUp. Retrieved from - https://www.betterup.com/blog/leading-by-example
3. Center for Creative Leadership. (n.d.). Authenticity: 1 idea, 3 facts, 5 tips. CCL. Retrieved from - https://www.ccl.org/articles/leading-effectively-articles/authenticity-1-idea-3-facts-5-tips/
4. Corporate Finance Institute. (n.d.). Leading by example. Corporate Finance Institute. Retrieved from - https://corporatefinanceinstitute.com/resources/management/leading-by-example/
5. Diversio. (n.d.). What role should leadership teams play in DEI? Diversio. Retrieved from - https://diversio.com/what-role-should-leadership-teams-play-in-dei/
6. Fingerprint for Success. (n.d.). Leading by example. Fingerprint for Success. Retrieved from - https://www.fingerprintforsuccess.com/blog/leading-by-example
7. Forbes Coaches Council. (2018, March 13). Seven ways to develop your authentic leadership style. Forbes. Retrieved from - https://www.forbes.com/sites/forbescoachescouncil/2018/03/13/seven-ways-to-develop-your-authentic-leadership-style/?sh=376c7bf569e6
8. Harappa Education. (n.d.). Authentic leadership: Examples, theory, and model. Harappa Education. Retrieved from - https://harappa.education/harappa-diaries/authentic-leadership-examples-theory-and-model/

9. Harvard Business School Online. (n.d.). Authentic leadership. HBS Online. Retrieved from -

   https://online.hbs.edu/blog/post/authentic-leadership

10. Indeed. (n.d.). Authentic leadership. Indeed. Retrieved from -

    https://www.indeed.com/career-advice/career-development/authentic-leadership

11. Jef Menguin. (n.d.). Lead by example. Jef Menguin. Retrieved from -

    https://jefmenguin.com/lead-by-example/

12. MindMeister. (n.d.). 7 reasons you should involve your team in decision-making. MindMeister. Retrieved from -

    https://www.mindmeister.com/blog/7-reasons-you-should-involve-your-team-in-decision-making/

13. MindTools. (n.d.). Leading by example. MindTools. Retrieved from -

    https://www.mindtools.com/aeouk1j/leading-by-example

14. Natural Talent. (n.d.). How to develop authentic leadership. Natural Talent. Retrieved from -

    https://www.natural-talent.com/en/blog/post/how-to-develop-authentic-leadership1

15. Runn. (n.d.). How to lead by example. Runn. Retrieved from -

    https://www.runn.io/blog/how-to-lead-by-example

16. Skillcast. (n.d.). Authentic leadership steps. Skillcast. Retrieved from -

    https://www.skillcast.com/blog/authentic-leadership-steps

17. Slack. (2019). Diversity at Slack. Slack. Retrieved from -

    https://slack.com/blog/news/diversity-at-slack-2019

18. Slack. (n.d.). Diversity at Slack. Slack. Retrieved from -

    https://slack.com/blog/news/diversity-at-slack-2

19. Strategic HR Inc. (n.d.). Inclusive decision-making principles. Strategic HR Inc. Retrieved from -

    https://strategichrinc.com/inclusive-decision-making-principles/

20. The Atlantic. (2018). How Slack got ahead in diversity. The Atlantic. Retrieved from -

    https://www.theatlantic.com/technology/archive/2018/04/how-slack-got-ahead-in-diversity/558806/

21. The Conference Board. (n.d.). Inclusive decision-making: Better results. The Conference Board. Retrieved from --

    https://www.conference-board.org/brief/corporate-citizenship/Inclusive-Decision-Making-Better-Results

22. ThoughtExchange. (n.d.). Employee involvement in decision-making. ThoughtExchange. Retrieved from -

    https://thoughtexchange.com/blog/employee-involvement-decision-making/

23. Tricentis. (n.d.). Inclusive decision-making. Tricentis. Retrieved from-

    https://www.tricentis.com/blog/inclusive-decision-making

24. Upskillist Pro. (n.d.). Should you always involve your team in decision-making? Upskillist Pro. Retrieved from -

    https://www.upskillist.pro/blog/should-you-always-involve-your-team-in-decision-making/

25. Western Governors University. (n.d.). What is authentic leadership? WGU. Retrieved from -

    https://www.wgu.edu/blog/what-is-authentic-leadership2004.html

Embodying Authentic Leadership

Mastering Inclusive Leadership

Chapter 6
Recognizing and Navigating Challenges

"In the midst of chaos, there is also opportunity."

Sun Tzu, Ancient China

Section 1: Introduction: Charting a Course Through Resistance in DEI Initiatives

Welcome to a pivotal chapter in our journey towards improving DEI in the workplace. This section is dedicated to empowering you with the tools and knowledge needed to identify and navigate the often-challenging waters of resistance to DEI initiatives. In an environment where skepticism and inertia can hinder progress, understanding how to maintain momentum and commitment to these essential efforts is crucial.

Overcoming Barriers: Knowledge as Power

Our exploration begins with a comprehensive understanding of the common hurdles faced in DEI implementation. Resistance in the workplace can stem from a variety of sources, from deep-rooted biases and a lack of understanding to a fear of change and perceived threats to the status quo. By identifying these barriers, you'll gain insight into the psychology and dynamics at play, enabling you to craft effective strategies to address and overcome them.

Navigating Skepticism: Strategies for Success

Skepticism can be a formidable opponent in the pursuit of a more inclusive and equitable workplace. This stage will guide you through the nuances of addressing doubts and concerns and converting skepticism into engagement and support. You'll learn how to articulate the value of DEI in a language that resonates with various stakeholders, turning potential obstacles into opportunities for dialogue and growth.

Sustaining Momentum: Tools for Long-Term Success

Equally important is maintaining the momentum of your DEI initiatives. This component will provide you with practical tools and methodologies to ensure that DEI efforts are not just a fleeting trend but a sustainable and integral part of your organizational culture. From setting achievable goals to monitoring progress and celebrating milestones, you'll discover how to keep the DEI flame burning brightly in your organization.

A Process of Collective Growth

Remember, the path to a truly equitable, welcoming, and diverse atmosphere is a collective voyage. It's about building bridges, opening dialogues, and creating spaces where all voices are heard and valued. This guidance is designed not just to instruct but to inspire—to turn challenges into catalysts for change and growth.

Let's embrace the challenge and turn the tide on resistance while charting a course towards a more inclusive workplace where everyone thrives.

Section 2: Embracing Diversity for Organizational Success

Leading the Way: Models of Excellence

Spotlight on Success: Shark Ninja and Allies

SharkNinja stands out with its broad-based hiring practices and global DEI advisory board. The company also boasts numerous employee resource groups (ERGs) and education initiatives (Built In, 2023). Similarly, ADP, through its involvement in the OneTen coalition, focuses on career advancement for Black talent and also operates various employee-led resource groups (Built In, 2023).

Ally Financial: Pioneering Equity

Ally Financial is another notable example, offering services like savings accounts and wealth management. They have implemented bias training for leadership and maintain equitable pay standards across positions, ensuring more than 40 percent of employees engage with their resource groups (Built In, 2023).

The Inclusive Innovators: UL Solutions and Accenture

UL Solutions, specializing in safety science, showcases diversity through its various business resource groups, including the Disability Alliance and Women in Leadership groups. It also has a Diversity + Inclusion Executive Council for strategic guidance (Built In, 2023). Accenture, a global consulting firm, takes strides in DEI with mandatory antiracism and unconscious bias training, along with a strong focus on gender balance and support for the LGBTQ+ community (Built In, 2023).

These companies' example of excellence serves as a call to action. It is a reminder that when organizations lead with empathy, equity, and inclusivity, they pave the way for a brighter, more inclusive future for all.

Section 3: Benefits of a Diverse and Inclusive Environment

Companies with strong DEI practices witness improved revenue, access to a broader pool of talent, higher employee engagement, and better retention rates (Top Workplaces, 2022). Furthermore, inclusive and varied workplaces are linked to a 12% increase in productivity and a 1.7-fold rise in innovation levels (Engagedly, n.d.).

Charting the Impact of DEI

- **Revenue Growth:** Companies with effective DEI programs often see higher revenue due to increased employee effort and dedication.
- **Talent Acquisition:** A wider recruitment scope allows for tapping into a more diverse talent pool.
- **Employee Engagement:** Culturally diverse workplaces enhance employee connection and engagement.

Mastering Inclusive Leadership

- **Retention Rates:** Diversity practices lead to higher loyalty and reduced turnover.
- **Productivity and Innovation:** A significant uptick in productivity and innovation is observed in companies embracing DEI.

Driving Factors Behind Successful DEI Initiatives

- **Leadership Commitment:** Strong DEI programs start with top-level endorsement and active participation.
- **Employee Resource Groups:** These groups build a sense of belonging and facilitate personal and professional growth.
- **Comprehensive Training:** Antiracism and unconscious bias training are vital for creating a collaborative culture.
- **Equitable Practices:** Fair compensation and transparent promotion processes are key.

Dynamic Benefits of DEI	Impactful Outcomes and Strategies	Common Criticisms	Response to Criticisms
Revenue Enhancement	Companies with strong DEI practices often see higher revenue due to increased employee effort and dedication (Top Workplaces, 2022).	Doubt over DEI's direct impact on revenue.	Empirical evidence shows a correlation between diverse workforces and higher revenue, likely due to a broader range of perspectives leading to better decision-making and market understanding (Top Workplaces, 2022).
Talent Pool Expansion	A broader recruitment scope in DEI-friendly companies taps into a more diverse talent pool (Top Workplaces, 2022).	Concerns that diversity hinders talent quality.	Studies indicate that diverse talent pools contribute to a range of skills and experiences, enhancing the quality and versatility of the workforce (Top Workplaces, 2022).

Recognizing and Navigating Challenges

Boost in Engagement	Inclusive workplaces enhance employee connection and engagement (Top Workplaces, 2022).	Questioning the link between inclusion and engagement.	Research has consistently shown that employees in workplaces that are accessible feel more valued and motivated, directly impacting their engagement and productivity (Top Workplaces, 2022).
Improved Retention	Diversity practices lead to higher loyalty and reduced turnover (Top Workplaces, 2022).	Skepticism about diversity's role in retention.	Diverse and welcoming environments address employee needs more holistically, leading to higher satisfaction and retention (Top Workplaces, 2022).
Innovation Uptick	Companies embracing DEI see a significant increase in productivity and innovation (Engagedly, n.d.).	Doubts on how diversity drives innovation.	Diversity brings varied perspectives, which are crucial for innovative thinking and problem-solving, leading to more creative outcomes (Engagedly, n.d.).

Section 4: Spotting Roadblocks: How to Understand Obstacles

Real-World Example: Overcoming Challenges in DEI

Thoughtworks, a global software consultancy, exemplifies an organization that successfully integrated DEI into its core mission. This inclusion not only distinguished the company but also significantly supported its social and economic objectives (Quantive, n.d.). Thoughtworks' approach underscores the importance of integrating DEI into an organization's overarching goals and values.

Types of Resistance in DEI Implementation

When deploying DEI principles, various forms of resistance can arise. These can be broadly categorized into:

- Lack of a Measurable Strategy: Often, DEI efforts are well-intentioned but lack a focused, trackable approach. Setting clear, measurable objectives using frameworks like R.A.C.E™ and/or Objectives and Key Results (OKRs) can align DEI with the organization's larger goals (Quantive, n.d.).

- Inadequate Resources: DEI initiatives often suffer from underfunding. Effective DEI leadership involves advocating for sufficient resources and gaining allies within the organization to support these efforts (Quantive, n.d.).

- Blind Spots: Even well-intentioned DEI leaders may have limited perspectives. Regular discussions with diverse employee groups are crucial to gain broad insights and minimize these blind spots (Quantive, n.d.).

- Perceived Lack of Urgency: DEI is often seen as important but not urgent. This perception changes only when a crisis occurs. To avoid this, DEI should be framed as essential for the organization's well-being (Quantive, n.d.).

- Implicit Biases: Unconscious biases can significantly hinder DEI integration. Training sessions focused on recognizing and addressing these biases are essential for creating a more objective decision-making environment (Quantive, n.d.).

Early Identification and Training Solutions

Recognizing these challenges early is vital for the successful implementation of DEI. Targeted training solutions, such as workshops and digital training formats, can effectively change attitudes and behaviors towards DEI (Affirmity, 2021). Interactive workshops deliver impactful diversity messages, promoting an attitude of inclusion at every organizational level.

Identifying and overcoming obstacles in DEI implementation is a complex process that requires strategic planning, resource allocation, continuous evaluation, and tailored training programs. By anticipating common challenges and adopting a proactive approach, organizations can effectively integrate DEI into their culture and operations.

Recognizing and Navigating Challenges

Challenges in DEI Strategies	Overview and Solutions	Common Skepticism	Responses to Skepticism
Strategic Planning in DEI	Lack of a measurable strategy can derail DEI efforts. Implementing frameworks like OKRs ensures alignment with organizational goals and provides a trackable approach (Quantive, n.d.).	Doubt over the effectiveness of structured frameworks in DEI.	Using structured frameworks like R.A.C.E.™ and/or OKRs has been shown to offer clear direction and measurable outcomes in DEI, proving their effectiveness in aligning efforts with broader organizational goals (Quantive, n.d.).
Resource Allocation for DEI	DEI initiatives often face underfunding. Effective leadership must advocate for adequate resources and cultivate internal support (Quantive, n.d.).	Concerns about the feasibility of acquiring sufficient funding for DEI initiatives.	Success stories from groups that successfully pushed for and got the resources they needed show that, with strong leadership, getting money for DEI projects is possible and can have a big effect (Quantive, n.d.).
Addressing DEI Blind Spots	Limited perspectives of DEI leaders can lead to blind spots. Engaging in regular dialogues with diverse employee groups provides broader insights and helps minimize these blind spots (Quantive, n.d.).	Belief that DEI leaders can fully understand and address all aspects of diversity on their own.	Regular interactions with diverse groups within the organization have proven essential in broadening leaders' perspectives and effectively addressing DEI blind spots (Quantive, n.d.).
Urgency in DEI Implementation	DEI is often not seen as urgent until a crisis occurs. Framing DEI as essential for organizational well-being can elevate its perceived importance (Quantive, n.d.).	DEI is viewed as a secondary concern, not requiring immediate action.	When you talk about DEI as an important part of an organization's health and success, it seems more important, and research shows that proactive DEI efforts improve the organization's results, which goes against the idea that it is not important (Quantive, n.d.).

		Implicit biases hinder DEI integration.		While training is not a standalone solution, it is a critical component
Combating Implicit Biases in DEI		Training focused on recognizing and addressing these biases creates a more objective decision-making environment (Quantive, n.d.).	Training alone is insufficient to change deep-seated biases.	in raising awareness and initiating behavioral changes, thus playing a significant role in mitigating biases and cultivating inclusivity (Quantive, n.d.).

Section 5: Change the Course: Strategies to Overcome Skepticism

BMe Community's Positive Shift in DEI Narrative

The BMe Community, under the direction of author and CEO Trabian Shorters, provides a convincing example of how to successfully change a negative narrative surrounding DEI. This network of leaders and innovators shifted the focus from problem-centric to aspiration-centric, changing how marginalized employees and communities are perceived. Instead of labeling a young person in a high-crime area as 'at-risk,' BMe Community redefines them as a 'student,' emphasizing their aspirations and contributions. This asset framing approach, which moves away from viewing people as disadvantaged or underprivileged, has proven effective in changing the negative narrative surrounding DEI initiatives (Comnetworkdei.org, n.d.).

Tips to Turn Skepticism Into Buy-In

- **Emphasize Asset Framing:** By focusing on the positive contributions and aspirations of employees, organizations can transform the way they perceive and communicate about diverse groups, stimulating a more accessible environment.

- **Cultural Shift in Perspective:** It's crucial to move beyond superficial diversity metrics and aim for a cultural change that embeds DEI into every aspect of the organization. This involves transitioning from mandatory diversity training to a holistic approach that encourages each person to own and enrich the culture (Thinkupconsulting.com, 2020).

- **Engagement and Alignment:** Organizations should strive for alignment between their unique needs and a clear, DEI-driven vision. This approach involves understanding the roles people play in bringing this vision to life and developing cultural programs that reinforce and promote the identified goals and strategies.
- **Involvement of All Levels:** In a DEI-driven culture, everyone is responsible for living out the values and strategy. This means talent selection, training, and ongoing coaching are pivotal in enabling everyone to contribute effectively to the organization.

Buy-In Behaviors	Context	Counterarguments	Data-Informed Rebuttals
Positive Reinforcement Through Asset Framing	Focusing on one's positive contributions and aspirations allows organizations to perceive and communicate about diverse groups in a more pluralistic way (Comnetworkdei.org, n.d.).	Skepticism about the impact of asset framing on actual organizational change.	Asset framing has been shown to significantly alter perceptions, leading to more democratic behaviors and attitudes, proving its effectiveness in organizational change (Comnetworkdei.org, n.d.).
Beyond Metrics: Cultural DEI Integration	Aiming for a cultural shift that embeds DEI into every organization aspect is vital. This requires moving from mere mandatory training to a holistic culture of ownership and enrichment of DEI principles (Thinkupconsulting.com, 2020).	Doubts about the feasibility of integrating DEI deeply into organizational culture.	Demonstrated successes in companies that have deeply integrated DEI into their culture show that such an approach is not only feasible but also effective in creating lasting change (Thinkupconsulting.com, 2020).

Alignment with Organizational Vision	According to Thinkupconsulting.com (2020), aligning DEI initiatives with an organization's particular needs and vision ensures that everyone is aware of their contributions to making this vision a reality.	Questioning the practicality of aligning DEI initiatives with every organization's unique vision.	Practical examples of organizations successfully aligning DEI with their specific visions suggest that such alignment is not only practical but also enhances the relevance and impact of DEI initiatives (Thinkupconsulting.com, 2020).
All-Level Involvement in DEI	In a DEI-driven culture, responsibility lies with everyone, from leadership to individual employees. Talent selection, training, and ongoing coaching are crucial for enabling effective contribution to the organization's DEI goals (Thinkupconsulting.com, 2020).	Concerns about the practical implementation of involving all organizational levels in DEI initiatives.	Evidence from organizations that have successfully involved all levels in DEI initiatives indicates that such thorough involvement is not only practical but crucial for the success of DEI efforts (Thinkupconsulting.com, 2020).

Overcoming Common Misconceptions

Addressing and dispelling common misconceptions about DEI is essential. Many view DEI as a political issue or believe that embracing it means someone else must lose. It's vital to communicate that DEI benefits everyone, regardless of their background. DEI is about acknowledging and appreciating the diversity of identities and experiences, encouraging openness to different perspectives and truths (Lanereport.com, 2021).

By implementing these strategies, organizations can effectively change the narrative around DEI, turning skepticism into active support and creating an environment that is truly fair and equitable.

Recognizing and Navigating Challenges

Section 6: Keep the Ball Rolling: How to Maintain DEI Efforts Over Time

An Example of Sustained DEI Success

Paycor, a company offering cloud-based Human Capital Management software, demonstrates how to not only implement but also sustain successful DEI initiatives. Their "Perspectives+" initiative includes a range of resources like articles, templates, webinars, and practical tips, contributing to a diverse workplace culture. This program has helped Paycor garner recognition in several Top Workplaces awards over consecutive years (Top Workplaces, 2022).

Strategies for Long-Term DEI Commitment

- **Consistent Leadership Support:** Organizational leaders must consistently support DEI efforts in order for them to be successful. This involves not just initial implementation but ongoing commitment and visibility in DEI-related activities and discussions.

- **Embedding DEI into the Organizational Culture:** DEI should be part of the company's DNA, influencing policies, practices, and everyday interactions. This approach ensures that DEI is not seen as a one-off initiative but as an integral part of the organizational ethos.

- **Regular Monitoring and Reporting:** Keeping track of progress through regular monitoring and reporting helps maintain focus on DEI goals and highlights areas needing improvement or adjustment.

- **Employee Involvement and Resource Groups:** Encouraging employee participation in DEI initiatives and supporting resource groups catered to various demographics produces an inclusive environment where diverse voices are heard and valued.

- **Ongoing Training and Development:** Regular training programs, including refresher courses and updates on DEI topics, are crucial for keeping the momentum going. These programs should evolve to reflect current societal changes and internal organizational needs.

- **Quarterly Check-Ins and Feedback Loops:** Regular check-ins provide opportunities for employees to share their experiences and for

Mastering Inclusive Leadership

leadership to receive feedback. This open dialogue ensures that DEI efforts remain relevant and effective.

Training Programs for Ongoing DEI Efforts

DEI training should be an ongoing process, not a one-time event. Programs should include:

- Refresher courses to keep DEI principles at the forefront.
- Updates on new DEI topics reflect evolving societal and organizational contexts.
- Quarterly check-ins to assess the effectiveness of DEI initiatives and gather employee feedback.

By following these strategies and committing to continuous learning and development in DEI, organizations can ensure that their DEI efforts are not just temporary but are ingrained in their corporate culture, contributing to long-term success and sustainability.

Section 7: Recap of Chapter 6: Navigating the DEI Landscape

In Chapter 6, we set out on a trip through the expansive world of DEI. Here's a brief recap of the crucial points we covered:

- **Identifying Challenges:** We started by examining real-world examples of organizations like Thoughtworks that faced and overcame challenges in implementing DEI. We explored various types of resistance to DEI, such as a lack of measurable strategy, inadequate resources, and pervasive implicit biases.

- **Overcoming Skepticism:** Moving forward, we explored strategies to convert skepticism into active support. We learned from the transformative story of the BMe Community, which successfully shifted the negative narrative around DEI to a more positive and aspirational one.

- **Maintaining Momentum:** Finally, we discussed the importance of keeping the momentum alive for long-term DEI success. Companies like Paycor serve as exemplars in sustaining DEI efforts through

Recognizing and Navigating Challenges

continuous leadership support, embedding DEI into organizational culture, and ongoing training and development.

Synopsis	Synopsis of DEI Implementation	Potential Objections	Evidence-Based Rebuttals
DEI Success in Action	Paycor's "Perspectives+" initiative, a wide-ranging DEI program including resources like articles and webinars, has fostered a diverse culture and earned multiple Top Workplaces awards (Top Workplaces, 2022).	Doubts about the effectiveness of detailed DEI programs.	Paycor's consistent recognition in Top Workplaces awards validates the effectiveness of their extensive DEI approach (Top Workplaces, 2022).
Overcoming DEI Challenges	Thoughtworks exemplifies addressing DEI challenges like lack of measurable strategy and implicit biases, showcasing resilience in DEI progress (Top Workplaces, 2022).	Critique that DEI efforts are often superficial.	Thoughtworks' success in tackling specific challenges demonstrates a deep-rooted commitment to DEI, going beyond superficial efforts (Top Workplaces, 2022).
Transforming DEI Narratives	BMe Community's shift from negative to positive DEI narratives shows the power of positive framing in transforming skepticism into support (Comnetworkdei.org, n.d.).	Belief that narrative shifts are insufficient for organizational DEI change.	BMe Community's approach proves that changing narratives can lay the groundwork for deeper, systemic changes in DEI (Comnetworkdei.org, n.d.).

Sustaining DEI Momentum	Paycor's strategies for maintaining DEI momentum include continuous leadership support and integration of DEI into organizational culture (Top Workplaces, 2022).	Concerns about DEI efforts losing momentum over time.	Paycor's ongoing commitment and integration of DEI into its culture demonstrate how to maintain genuine momentum and avoid tokenistic efforts (Top Workplaces, 2022).

Preview of Chapter 7: Celebrating Victories in DEI

With a solid understanding of how to navigate the challenges and sustain momentum in DEI efforts, it's time to shift our focus to celebrating victories. In Chapter 7, we will illuminate the inspiring success stories from organizations that have not only embraced DEI but made it a lasting part of their culture. This portion of the book promises to be a treasure trove of practical tools and strategies, offering insights and guidance to help you effectively integrate DEI into your organization's fabric. Let's continue to learn, grow, and make meaningful changes together as we move beyond '**Compliance to Community'™**. **#WeNotMe**

References

1. Aperian Global. (n.d.). Winning over DEI skeptics. Retrieved from - https://aperian.com/blog/winning-over-dei-skeptics/
2. BizJournals. (2021, August 4). 9 effective ways to maintain the momentum of your DEI efforts. Retrieved from - https://www.bizjournals.com/bizjournals/news/2021/08/04/9-effective-ways-to-maintain-the-momentum-of-your-dei-efforts.html
3. eLearning Industry. (n.d.). 8 key aspects that will help you create effective DEI training programs for your organization. Retrieved from- https://www.eidesign.net/8-key-aspects-that-will-help-you-create-effective-dei-training-programs-for-your-organization/
4. Engagedly. (n.d.). 5 companies embracing diversity and inclusion through initiatives. Retrieved from - https://engagedly.com/blog/5-companies-embracing-diversity-and-inclusion-through-initiatives/
5. Entrepreneur. (n.d.). Know a DEI skeptic? Use these 3 strategies to engage them. Retrieved from - https://www.entrepreneur.com/growing-a-business/know-a-dei-skeptic-use-these-3-strategies-to-engage-them/457036
6. Fast Company. (2021, July 29). Entrepreneurs share 9 companies with admirable DEI efforts. Retrieved from - https://www.fastcompany.com/90690943/entrepreneurs-share-9-companies-with-admirable-dei-efforts
7. Forbes Coaches Council. (2021, September 24). 13 ways to maintain long-term momentum with DEI initiatives. Retrieved from - https://www.forbes.com/sites/forbescoachescouncil/2021/09/24/13-ways-to-maintain-long-term-momentum-with-dei-initiatives/?sh=711760274dfb

8. Harvard Business Review. (2022, November). To sustain DEI momentum, companies must invest in 3 areas. Retrieved from -

   https://hbr.org/2022/11/to-sustain-dei-momentum-companies-must-invest-in-3-areas

9. HR Dive. (n.d.). How to overcome employee resistance to DEI efforts. Retrieved from -

   https://www.hrdive.com/news/how-to-overcome-employee-resistance-to-dei-efforts/610119/

10. HR Dive. (n.d.). 7 ways to get exec buy-in for diversity and inclusion work. Retrieved from -

    https://www.hrdive.com/spons/7-ways-to-get-exec-buy-in-for-diversity-and-inclusion-work/617692/

11. HRU Group. (n.d.). DEI is still important: Here's how to maintain momentum. Retrieved from -

    https://hrugroup.com/blog/f/dei-is-still-important-here%E2%80%99s-how-to-maintain-momentum

12. JD Supra. (n.d.). Top 5 DEI challenges in the workplace. Retrieved from -

    https://www.jdsupra.com/legalnews/top-5-dei-challenges-in-the-workplace-9231342/

13. LinkedIn. (n.d.). What challenges implementing DEI program & how to overcome. Retrieved from -

    https://www.linkedin.com/pulse/what-challenges-implementing-dei-program-how-overcome-collier

14. Penn State Extension. (n.d.). Diversity training in the workplace. Retrieved from -

    https://extension.psu.edu/diversity-training-in-the-workplace

15. Quantive. (n.d.). DEI challenges. Retrieved from https://quantive.com/resources/articles/dei-challenges

16. RW-3. (n.d.). How to overcome resistance to DEI training. Retrieved from -

Recognizing and Navigating Challenges

https://www.rw-3.com/blog/how-to-overcome-resistance-to-dei-training

17. Sling. (n.d.). Diversity and inclusion training. Retrieved from -

    https://getsling.com/blog/diversity-and-inclusion-training/

18. SocialTalent. (n.d.). 9 companies around the world that are embracing diversity. Retrieved from -

    https://www.socialtalent.com/blog/diversity-and-inclusion/9-companies-around-the-world-that-are-embracing-diversity

19. TeamBuilding. (n.d.). DEI companies. Retrieved from -

    https://teambuilding.com/blog/dei-companies

20. The Diversity Movement. (n.d.). Ways to navigate DEI fatigue, maintain momentum, re-energize, re-invest. Retrieved from -

    https://thediversitymovement.com/ways-to-navigate-dei-fatigue-maintain-momentum-re-energize-re-invest/

21. Training & Development. (n.d.). How to challenge resistance to DEI initiatives. Retrieved from -

    https://www.td.org/atd-blog/how-to-challenge-resistance-to-dei-initiatives

Mastering Inclusive Leadership

Chapter 7
Applying Theory

"Diversity is a fact, but inclusion is a choice we make every day. As leaders, we have to put out the message that we embrace and not just tolerate diversity."

— Nellie Borrero, Managing Director, Global Inclusion & Diversity at Accenture

In this chapter, we will explore insights and tools that can drive change within your organization. You will gain access to a variety of exercises and assessments that translate the lessons learned from Cisco's experiences into steps. The goal is to bridge the gap between theory and practice, empowering you to implement DEI strategies in your workplace.

Prepare to be inspired by real-life success stories and discover how you can apply these narratives to your situation. This chapter serves as a call to action, motivating you to participate in implementing DEI initiatives and make an impact as a leader in your professional environment.

Section 1: Cisco's Robust DEI Framework - A Model of Success

Cisco's Exemplary Path in DEI: A Blueprint for Progress

Cisco, a player in the global tech industry, has become a model for DEI principles. Their comprehensive approach does not enrich their culture. Also contributes significantly to social and economic progress (Cisco, n.d.; CSRWire, n.d.). This chapter explores Cisco's strategies and practices regarding DEI, providing a blueprint for leaders seeking inspiration tailored to their specific circumstances.

Mastering Inclusive Leadership

As we delve into Cisco's journey to promoting DEI, we will uncover the benefits that an effective strategy brings. Both culturally and financially. Let's examine how Cisco sets the standard for embracing DEI principles and observe its impact on their organization.

Leading by Example: Cisco's Approach to Diversity, Equity and Inclusion

Cisco has established itself as a pioneer in the industry by implementing a framework for promoting DEI. Through programs and initiatives, Cisco prioritizes creating a work environment where every team member is valued and included. This commitment not only enhances Cisco's culture but also contributes to their broader social and economic goals (Cisco, n.d.; CSRWire, n.d.).

Dissecting Cisco's DEI Approach: A Detailed Exploration

Cisco's DEI Framework: Building an Inclusive Culture

Cisco's approach to DEI exemplifies a comprehensive and dynamic strategy, integrating these values deeply within its corporate fabric.

Comprehensive Inclusion Strategy

- Key Focus: Cisco's DEI framework goes beyond assembling a workforce; it aims to cultivate an inclusive environment where every team member feels valued and included. This strategy involves creating an ecosystem that embraces and appreciates differences while fostering a sense of belonging for all (Cisco, n.d.).

- Integration with Core Values: At Cisco, DEI is not treated as an agenda but integrated into the company's core values. This ensures that it remains a part of every decision and process.

Programs and Initiatives

- Wide Range of Initiatives: Cisco has implemented DEI initiatives consisting of programs tailored to address specific aspects of diversity and inclusion. These include recruitment strategies focused on diversity, cultural competence training programs, community engagement initiatives and leadership development programs emphasizing inclusivity (CSRWire, n.d.).

Applying Theory

- Long term Dedication: These programs exemplify Cisco's commitment to DEI, going beyond efforts and integrating these principles into the core of their operations.

Economic and Social Objectives

- Positive Impacts: The initiatives undertaken by Cisco in the realm of DEI have not only enriched their culture but have also made significant contributions to their social and economic objectives. Recognizing the value of having a diverse workforce, Cisco believes that diversity fosters creativity, improves problem solving capabilities and ultimately drives performance. (Cisco, n.d.; CSRWire, n.d.).

- Employee Satisfaction: By prioritizing DEI, Cisco has also observed outcomes in terms of employee retention and satisfaction, proving that these efforts yield benefits.

Impact Area	Evidence or Data Point	Counterpoints or Counterarguments	Business Benefit
Cisco's DEI Blueprint	Cisco's comprehensive DEI strategy, which includes a range of inclusive programs, has significantly contributed to its cultural and financial success. Their approach interweaves DEI with core values, emphasizing a sense of belonging (Cisco, n.d.; CSRWire, n.d.).	Skepticism about the real impact of DEI on business performance.	Cisco's experience shows tangible benefits in both employee satisfaction and economic performance, demonstrating that DEI initiatives can indeed have a substantial positive impact on businesses (Cisco, n.d.; CSRWire, n.d.).
Inclusivity as Core Strategy	Cisco's focus extends beyond building a workforce; they also prioritize nurturing an environment where each team member feels valued. This approach plays a role in their decision making process as an organization (Cisco, n.d.).	There are some concerns regarding how effective it's to integrate DEI into core business strategies.	Cisco's successful integration of DEI into its core values and decision making processes proves that this approach can greatly enhance culture and performance (Cisco, n.d.).

Diverse Initiatives for Different Needs	Cisco's DEI initiatives are tailored to address specific aspects of diversity and inclusion, including recruitment, training, and leadership development (CSRWire, n.d.).	Questioning the need for a wide array of DEI initiatives.	Cisco has implemented a range of DEI initiatives that specifically target aspects of diversity and inclusion, such as recruitment, training and leadership development (CSRWire, n.d.). This showcases the importance of having a set of initiatives to effectively address the complexities associated with DEI (CSRWire, n.d.).
Long-Term Commitment and Impact	Cisco's focus extends beyond building a workforce; they also prioritize nurturing an environment where each team member feels valued. This approach plays a role in their decision making process as an organization (Cisco, n.d.). (Cisco, n.d.; CSRWire, n.d.).	Belief that DEI efforts are often short-lived and don't lead to long-term benefits.	What sets Cisco apart is its long term commitment to DEI. They go beyond efforts by embedding these principles into their operations, which has an impact on employee retention and satisfaction (Cisco, n.d.; CSRWire, n.d.). This challenges the belief that DEI efforts are often short lived and fail to generate long term benefits.
Economic and Social Synergy through DEI	Recognizing the value of having a workforce Cisco believes that diversity fosters creativity, improves problem solving capabilities and ultimately drives performance.	Perception that DEI initiatives are more about social responsibility than business benefits.	Cisco's experience highlights that DEI is not just a social responsibility but a strategic business approach, leading to improved problem-solving, creativity, and financial outcomes (Cisco, n.d.; CSRWire, n.d.).

Section 2: Wins Worth Sharing - Real Success Stories in DEI Training

Narratives of Triumph: DEI Training Successes Across Industries

Adaptability and Influence Across Industries

Now let's examine how successful implementation of DEI training has occurred across sectors and organizations of all sizes. From technology companies to non-profit organizations, DEI training has proven to be a key factor in success. Consider these examples:

- **Tech Sector:** A technology firm implemented DEI training, leading to enhanced team collaboration and innovation. The focus was on understanding broad perspectives, which resulted in improved problem-solving and product development (Harvard Business Publishing, n.d.).

- **Healthcare Industry:** In healthcare, a hospital embraced DEI training to better understand patient demographics. This led to improved patient care and stronger community engagement (Aperian Global, n.d.).

- **Retail Industry:** A retail chain introduced DEI initiatives to create a more inclusive shopping experience. This resulted in higher customer satisfaction and loyalty. Their training emphasized cultural sensitivity and inclusivity at the point of sale (Chief Learning Officer, 2020).

- **Manufacturing Industry:** A manufacturing company's DEI training focused on equitable practices in the workplace, resulting in a significant reduction in conflicts and an increase in employee satisfaction (Comstock's Magazine, n.d.).

Key Elements of Success in DEI Training

To effectively implement DEI training within your organization, it is crucial to consider the following aspects:

- Tailoring to Industry Needs: Customize the training program to specifically address the challenges and opportunities facing your industry.

Mastering Inclusive Leadership

- Leadership Engagement: Ensure participation and commitment from the leadership team in the training process.
- Ongoing Efforts: Remember, DEI training is not a one-time event but a continuous cycle towards improvement.

These narratives from culturally diverse industries demonstrate that DEI training, with the right approach and commitment, can lead to substantial positive changes in any organization. Reflect on how these principles can be adapted to your context to achieve similar successes.

Impact Area	Evidence or Data Point	Counterpoints or Counterexamples	Business Benefit
Revolutionizing Workplaces	Notable business transformation through focused DEI training enhances culture and employee relations (Harvard Business Publishing, n.d.).	Questioning the effectiveness of DEI training in real change.	Proven improvements in employee relations and the workplace environment validate the effectiveness of focused DEI training.
DEI Across Industries	Successful DEI implementation in the tech, healthcare, retail, and manufacturing sectors (Aperian Global, n.d.; Chief Learning Officer, 2020; Comstock's Magazine, n.d.)	Skepticism about DEI adaptability across different sectors.	Various sector examples demonstrate DEI's adaptability and positive impact on business outcomes.
Key Success Elements in DEI	. Emphasis on customization, leadership involvement, and ongoing efforts for effective DEI training.	Doubts about the practicality of DEI integration in business.	The success stories from various sectors show the practicality and positive outcomes of integrating DEI into business strategies.

Key Success Elements in DEI   Emphasis on customization, leadership involvement, and ongoing efforts for effective DEI training.
Doubts about the practicality of DEI integration in business.   The success stories from various sectors show the practicality and positive outcomes of integrating DEI into business strategies.

Applying Theory

Section 3: Your DEI Toolbox - Inclusive Leadership Toolkit

Equipping Leaders: Tools for DEI Implementation

Let's take a stroll through the global landscape of DEI implementation tools and think about how they can fit into your leadership style.

Think of DEI training as a self-assessment quiz reflecting not your appearance but your comprehension of DEI principles. This isn't about right or wrong answers; it's about discovering where you can grow. Reference step #1: 'Recognize' from the R.A.C.E.™ framework from my first book. (Harvard DEIB Explorer, n.d.; Washington College, n.d.; The Center at MSU, n.d.).

Now, think about role-play scenarios. It's like rehearsing for a play where every act is a real-life situation in your workplace. You get to try out different ways to handle DEI challenges in a safe space before the live show (SimInsights, n.d.; LinkedIn, n.d.; McLean & Company, n.d.).

Self-Assessment Quizzes

- Purpose: These quizzes are essential for leaders to evaluate their understanding of DEI and identify areas that need growth. The self-assessment approach offers a reflective space to pinpoint strengths and areas for improvement in DEI knowledge and application. Try one of the quizzes from Harvard DEIB Explorer that helps you reflect on your awareness of inclusion dynamics. It's about getting that insight into where you stand and where you can grow. (Harvard DEIB Explorer, n.d.; Washington College, n.d.; The Center at MSU, n.d.).

Role-Play Scenarios

- Application: Real-world scenarios are a practical way to understand DEI principles in action. These exercises provide leaders with situations where they can apply DEI strategies, offering a safe space to explore and practice their responses to various challenges. Think about a scenario from LinkedIn Learning where you navigate a difficult conversation about unconscious bias. These real-world situations allow you to practice your responses and develop your DEI skills in a safe environment. (SimInsights, n.d.; LinkedIn, n.d.; McLean & Company, n.d.).

DEI Action Plan Template

- Consider the DEI Action Plan Template as your personal roadmap. It's not a one-size-fits-all plan but a guide that you tailor to your organization's inclusive strategic goals and objectives. Try using a template from the National Parent-Teacher Association (PTA) to chart your organization's DEI path. It can serve as a guide, helping you establish goals and strategies for cultivating an inclusive culture. The National Parent Teacher Association (PTA), San Jose State University, and the University of Oregon Center for Creative Leadership offer resources in this regard. (PTA, n.d.; San Jose State University, n.d.; University of Oregon, n.d.; Center for Creative Leadership, n.d.).

Case Studies

- Case studies are like tales from fellow travelers on the DEI path. They're stories of triumphs and challenges that can inspire and guide you. Consider reading a case from Inklusiiv about a company that successfully integrated DEI into their core business strategy. These stories can serve as inspiration and a practical guide for your DEI journey. (Inklusiiv, n.d.; Communications Network DEI, n.d.).

Inclusive Meeting Checklist

- The Inclusive Meeting Checklist acts as a compass, ensuring that every team member's voice is heard and valued. Its purpose is to create an environment where diversity's not just present but actively embraced. Utilize a checklist from the University of Alaska Anchorage as a tool to guarantee that your meetings become spaces where every voice feels included. (University of Alaska Anchorage, n.d.; Harvard University, n.d.; Quiet Revolution, n.d.; SRC, n.d.).

Microaggression Awareness Guide

- The Microaggression Awareness Guide is your lens to spot both intended and unintended moments that can make or break an inclusive culture. Consider using a guide from Great Place to Work that helps you identify and address biases in everyday interactions. These resources are vital for creating respectful and inclusive work environments. (Great Place to Work, n.d.; Berlitz, n.d.; Forbes, 2017; Harvard Business Review, 2022; Baker College, n.d.; Forbes, 2020).

Applying Theory

Feedback and Feedforward

- Lastly, the feedback and feedforward cycles help you gauge how well your DEI efforts are resonating within your organization. Think about using a feedforward to highlight positive programs toward DEI goals while using feedback as the foundation for these insights.

- SurveyMonkey forms can provide crucial data points into how your DEI efforts are perceived within your organization. This could be a valuable tool for measuring the impact of your initiatives. (SurveyMonkey, n.d.; JotForm, n.d.; Formsite, n.d.; ProProfs Survey Maker, n.d.).

Resource List

The University of Washington Tacoma's Professional Development Center offers a rich collection of DEI resources tailored for enhancing workplace inclusivity. Their offerings include insightful articles and videos that can serve as practical tools for leaders at all levels.

The Communications Network (n.d.) provides an extensive array of DEI tools, focusing on communications for organizational change and racial equity. Their resources are designed to integrate DEI principles into your organization's strategic framework effectively.

WordStream (2022) presents a targeted list of DEI resources for small businesses, emphasizing inclusive marketing, language, and ethical business practices. This guide is particularly beneficial for integrating DEI strategies into small-scale operations.

Lastly, the **Council on Accreditation** (2020) outlines ten essential resources for your equity, diversity, and inclusion efforts, offering a foundational approach to fostering an inclusive organizational culture.

Together, these tools are like a Swiss Army knife for DEI—versatile, essential, and uniquely suited to your preferred leadership style. Use them to carve out a more inclusive and equitable space in your organization. By incorporating these insights and tools into your strategies, you can carve out an inclusive and equitable space within your company. This integration will drive change by enhancing both culture and external impact.

Impact Area	Evidence or Data Point	Counterpoints or Counterexamples	Business Benefit
Mirror of Growth: Self-Assessment Quizzes	It is essential for leaders to evaluate DEI understanding and identify growth areas, offering reflective insights (Harvard DEIB Explorer, n.d.; Washington College, n.d.; The Center at MSU, n.d.).	Doubts about the effectiveness of self-assessment in real-world applications.	The quizzes are specifically designed to highlight areas for DEI growth, enhancing self-awareness which is critical for effective leadership.
Rehearsing Inclusivity: Role-Play Scenarios	Practical scenarios for applying DEI strategies in a safe environment, improving real-life DEI skills (SimInsights, n.d.; LinkedIn, n.d.; McLean & Company, n.d.).	Questioning the impact of simulated scenarios on actual behavior.	Role-plays have been proven to enhance understanding and preparedness for handling sensitive DEI issues, reflecting real-life situations.
Navigating DEI: Action Plan Template	Guides for creating tailored DEI strategies help outline clear goals (PTA, n.d.; San Jose State University, n.d.; University of Oregon, n.d.).	Concerns about the one-size-fits-all nature of templates.	These templates are starting points meant to be adapted to each organization's unique DEI voyage.
Journeys of Change: Case Studies	Inspirational tales from organizations that integrated DEI into their strategy (Inklusiiv, n.d.; Communications Network DEI, n.d.).	Doubts about the applicability of other organizations' experiences.	These case studies provide a mixture of real-world examples of successful DEI integration, showcasing adaptable strategies.

Voice Equity: Inclusive Meeting Checklist	Ensures every voice is heard in meetings, promoting active engagement (University of Alaska Anchorage, n.d.; Harvard University, n.d.; Quiet Revolution, n.d.; SRC, n.d.).	Belief that checklists stifle natural conversation flow.	These checklists are designed to enhance inclusivity without compromising the spontaneity of discussions.
Spotting Subtlety: Microaggression Guide	Guides to identify and address workplace microaggressions, cultivating respect (Great Place to Work, n.d.; Berlitz, n.d.; Forbes, 2017; [Harvard Business Review, 2022] (https://hbr		

Section 4: Make It Fit - Tailoring DEI Training to Your Context

Adapting DEI Training: Customized Strategies for Impact

- Contextual Adaptation: The Key to Effective DEI Initiatives

    Imagine DEI leadership training as a custom-tailored suit. Just as a tailor adjusts the fabric to fit the unique contours of each individual, DEI training for leaders should be adapted to fit the specific cultural, industrial, and organizational contours of your workplace. This customization ensures that the leadership training resonates with your team, addressing the unique challenges and harnessing the unique opportunities within your environment.

- The Power of Bespoke DEI Training: A Case Study

    Sodexo, featured in the Social Talent article, provides an excellent example of bespoke DEI leader training. Sodexo's approach focuses on gender parity and has led to significant improvements in various areas of their business. They've achieved a notable gender balance in

Mastering Inclusive Leadership

their executive committee and board of directors, which has resulted in increased employee engagement, gross profit, and a stronger brand image. Additionally, Sodexo supports LGBTQ+ and ally employee networks, emphasizing community involvement and awareness.

This example demonstrates how tailored DEI initiatives, which respect and value multinational backgrounds, can significantly impact employee satisfaction and business outcomes. Sodexo's case is a robust model for leaders looking to integrate DEI effectively into their corporate culture. (Social Talent, n.d.).

Impact Area	Evidence or Data Point	Counterpoints or Counterexamples	Business Benefit
Custom-Fit DEI Training	DEI training should be tailored to fit the unique cultural, industrial, and organizational contours, ensuring relevance and effectiveness (Contextual Adaptation).	There are concerns about the feasibility of customizing DEI training for every organization.	Customization is key to effective DEI, as it addresses specific needs and challenges, enhancing impact and resonance within the organization.
Sodexo's DEI Success Story	Sodexo's bespoke DEI approach, focusing on gender parity and supporting LGBTQ+ networks, led to improved employee engagement, profit, and brand image (Social Talent, n.d.).	Doubts about the replicability of success in different organizational contexts.	Sodexo's success demonstrates the power of a tailored approach, proving that with careful planning and commitment, bespoke DEI strategies can be effective in various organizational environments.

Summary and What's Next
Consolidating Learnings and Looking Ahead

When reflecting on Chapter 7 of our discussion material, consider how the insights shared and strategies discussed can be applied to your leadership practices. Remember that it is not about possessing tools; it is about understanding when and how to effectively utilize them within your context. As we move forward together on this journey, get ready to explore the emerging trends in DEI.

Applying Theory

As we move forward, get ready to explore upcoming trends in DEI. The next chapter will educate, equip, and empower you with insights and foresight to navigate the evolving DEI landscape, ensuring your organization is not only keeping pace but leading the charge in creating a globally inclusive future as you continue your path toward organizational excellence by moving from **'Compliance to Community."** ¬ **#WeNotMe**

Chapter Seven Summary	Key Takeaways
Cisco's DEI Paradigm	Cisco exemplifies a holistic DEI strategy, integrating it deeply within its corporate culture and operations, impacting both its organizational culture and economic milestones.
Practical Insights and Tools	The chapter emphasizes translating Cisco's DEI learnings into practical, actionable strategies for readers to apply in their organizations.
Empowering DEI Implementation	Focuses on the empowerment and inspiration drawn from real-world success stories, encouraging effective DEI implementation in various professional environments.
Comprehensive Inclusion Strategy	Highlights Cisco's approach to creating an inclusive environment, valuing each team member, and integrating DEI with core company values.
Diverse DEI Initiatives	Cisco's comprehensive efforts in promoting DEI encompass initiatives such as targeted recruitment, training programs and leadership development. These initiatives are designed to address aspects of diversity and inclusion within the organization.
Impact on Business and Culture	Cisco's DEI strategy has been proven to have an impact on fronts. It fosters creativity, enhances problem solving capabilities, boosts employee satisfaction levels, and even contributes to performance. This demonstrates the influence that DEI can have on both the business environment and organizational culture.
Adaptability in DEI Leadership Training	The implementation of DEI training across sectors highlights its adaptability. Notable examples include its effectiveness in technology driven industries like tech, as healthcare, retail and manufacturing sectors.
Tailoring DEI to Organizational Needs	Emphasizes the importance of customizing DEI training to fit specific industry needs and organizational contexts, as illustrated by Sodexo's case study.

131

References

1. Berlitz. (n.d.). Examples of microaggressions in the workplace. Retrieved from -

   https://www.berlitz.com/blog/examples-microaggressions-workplace

2. Cisco. (n.d.). Inclusion & diversity. Retrieved from -

   https://www.cisco.com/c/en/us/about/inclusion-diversity.html

3. ComNetworkDEI. (n.d.). DEI resources. Retrieved from -

   https://www.comnetworkdei.org/dei-resources

4. ComNetworkDEI. (n.d.). Case studies. Retrieved from -

   https://www.comnetworkdei.org/casestudies

5. Council on Accreditation. (2020, October). 10 resources for your equity, diversity, and inclusion efforts. Retrieved from -

   https://coanet.org/2020/10/10-resources-for-your-equity-diversity-and-inclusion-efforts/

6. Formsite. (n.d.). Diversity training feedback survey template. Retrieved from -

   https://www.formsite.com/templates/survey-templates/diversity-training-feedback/

7. Forbes Coaches Council. (2017, March 7). How good leadership can minimize microaggressions. Retrieved from -

   https://www.forbes.com/sites/forbescoachescouncil/2017/03/07/how-good-leadership-can-minimize-microaggressions/?sh=6d11d9274d70

8. Great Place to Work. (n.d.). Microaggressions in the workplace: How to identify & respond to them. Retrieved from -

   https://www.greatplacetowork.com/resources/blog/microaggressions-in-the-workplace-how-to-identify-respond-to-them

9. Harvard Business Review. (2022, May). Recognizing and responding to microaggressions at work. Retrieved from -

   https://hbr.org/2022/05/recognizing-and-responding-to-microaggressions-at-work

10. Harvard University. (n.d.). Inclusive meeting guide. Retrieved from -

    https://edib.harvard.edu/files/dib/files/inclusive_meeting_guide_final_1.pdf?m=1617641674

11. Inklusiiv. (n.d.). DEI case studies. Retrieved from -

    https://inklusiiv.com/dei-case-studies/

12. JotForm. (n.d.). [Form title as appears on the page]. Retrieved from -

    https://form.jotform.com/200586814389061

13. ProProfs Survey Maker. (n.d.). Diversity, equity, and inclusion survey questions. Retrieved from -

    https://www.proprofssurvey.com/blog/diversity-equity-and-inclusion-survey-questions/

14. SurveyMonkey. (n.d.). DEI leader toolkit. Retrieved from -

    https://www.surveymonkey.com/toolkit/dei-leader/

15. Tacoma, University of Washington. (n.d.). DEI resources for your workplace. Retrieved from -

    https://www.tacoma.uw.edu/pdc/dei-resources

16. WordStream. (2022, May 31). Diversity, equity & inclusion resources. Retrieved from -

    https://www.wordstream.com/blog/ws/2022/05/31/diversity-equity-inclusion-resources

Mastering Inclusive Leadership

Chapter 8

Envisioning the Future

"A diverse mix of voices leads to better discussions, decisions, and outcomes for everyone."

- Sundar Pichai, CEO of Google

In this chapter, we delve into the trends and global impact of DEI. It's crucial to look at and understand how DEI is shaping up for the times. We'll uncover emerging trends in DEI and discuss how they could influence the world on a large scale. The aim is to equip leaders with insights into these changes in DEI and help them prepare for their impact worldwide.

By emphasizing the significance of leadership, we'll guide teams on how to adapt to shifts effectively, ensuring they can navigate a changing world landscape positively. This journey will reveal how embracing inclusive leadership practices can mold the future, empowering you and your team to face evolving challenges with flexibility and foresight.

Section 1: Innovative Leadership at Apple: A Closer Look at DEI Strategy

At the forefront of the changing narrative around diversity, equity and inclusion stands Apple as a symbol of innovation, not in technology but in cultivating an inclusive corporate environment.

Apple's DEI strategy revolves around maintaining an environment that promotes diversity across all levels of the organization while upholding accountability. Their initiatives include creating technology features that cater to employees who are deaf or hard of hearing, designing products that meet the needs of people from various backgrounds, and implementing programs that enhance opportunities for underrepresented groups. Moreover, Apple extends its support to veterans, acknowledges events and builds a sense of community through Diversity Network Associations. These tactics highlight the company's dedication to diversity, equity and inclusion, which play a role in its achievements by embracing varied perspectives and nurturing a sense of belonging.

Apple's comprehensive DEI framework, with its array of programs, serves as a blueprint for forward thinking strategies in this field. The company's endeavors, spanning global diversity initiatives to leadership programs, underline a commitment to creating an atmosphere where every person feels valued. Apple's success story underscores how aligning DEI with core business strategies can drive excellence and societal change effectively (Apple Report 2024; Diversity Impact Report 2024).

Apple's DEI Core	Implications for Practice
Understanding DEI's trajectory and its global implications is paramount for future leadership	Leaders need to keep up to date with developments in DEI and adjust their approaches to make sure their teams are ready for shifts.
Apple's DEI plan, centered on fostering an environment that boosts diversity in the workforce and promotes accountability, demonstrates the influence of purposeful DEI initiatives.	Organizations should consider adopting comprehensive and intentional DEI strategies similar to Apple's (Apple, 2024) to enhance their success and inclusivity.
Apple's initiatives highlight the importance of inclusivity in product design, community support, and celebrating cultural moments (Diversity for Social Impact, 2024).	Emphasizing inclusive product design and community engagement can foster a broader sense of belonging and contribute to an organization's overall DEI success.
Apple serves as a model for future-oriented DEI strategies, demonstrating how DEI can be aligned with core business strategies for societal impact and organizational excellence (Apple, 2024; Diversity for Social Impact, 2024).	Other organizations can draw inspiration from Apple's approach to integrating DEI into their business models, potentially leading to enhanced societal impact and organizational performance.

Envisioning the Future

Section 2: Getting Ready for the Future: Getting Prepared for Evolving Trends in Diversity, Equity and Inclusion

As we look ahead to the future, it is important to stay aware of the changing dynamics in DEI. New developments, like incorporating technology to promote inclusivity and focusing on intersectionality, are reshaping how DEI is approached. Adapting to these changes calls for a mindset that anticipates shifts and builds flexibility into DEI training programs. Organizations need to lead the way by using insights and innovations to ensure their DEI efforts are adaptable, up-to-date and consider a viewpoint.

The evolving societal norms, changing laws and ongoing organizational learning all play a role in shaping the DEI landscape. As noted in an article from People Managing People (2023), the political climate post-2016 has had an impact on how corporations address DEI issues, underscoring the importance of adaptability and resilience in DEI strategies (People Managing People, 2023). Understanding how social change cycles influence DEI initiatives is essential. The article emphasizes the significance of looking to challenges and opportunities in the DEI space, especially considering recent political and legal changes that have introduced new hurdles for DEI efforts in the business sector.

Section 3: Looking Beyond Boundaries: Getting Ready for Global Influence

DEI goes beyond borders, embodying a need that demands awareness and action. Training for inclusivity isn't just advantageous; it's crucial. As leaders, developing an understanding and respect for differences serves as the foundation of DEI endeavors. Incorporating practices for inclusivity, such as cultural sensitivity training and encouraging a culture of openness and curiosity, can boost your team's effectiveness in navigating diverse cultural environments.

Recognizing the Significance of Anticipation in DEI

The DEI landscape follows a pattern mirroring societal shifts and economic changes. Recent challenges like the induced "shecession" and varying levels of enthusiasm for DEI initiatives underscore the importance of resilience and flexibility in DEI strategies. The post affirmative action era and legislative shifts in states indicate the changing social environment within which DEI functions, underscoring the need to be ready for various outcomes and situations (People Managing People, 2023).

Section 4: Current Developments Influencing Diversity, Equity and Inclusion

A number of trends are influencing the direction of DEI in workplaces. Initially, there is a growing focus on embracing intersectionality within DEI efforts, recognizing the connections among identity factors (Loeb Leadership, 2023). Furthermore, the adoption of technology to promote hiring practices, such as utilizing AI to mitigate biases in recruitment processes, is becoming prevalent (Loeb Leadership, 2023).

The transition towards work has also paved the way for global inclusion by prompting organizations to establish diverse and inclusive virtual teams (Vantage Circle, 2023). Additionally, there is an increasing emphasis on addressing concerns within settings, according to the Forbes Human Resources Council (2023), linking DEI initiatives with broader environmental, social and governance (ESG) considerations. This trend mirrors a rising expectation from consumers and employees for companies to take a stance on issues by integrating DEI strategies into their core business operations.

Several significant trends are set to influence the landscape of DEI

Key Trends Shaping the Future of DEI	Implications for Practice
Technological Progress: Integrating AI and machine learning into diversity, equity and inclusion (DEI) initiatives will enhance the ability to address biases and promote practices.	Companies should use AI and machine learning tools to identify and mitigate biases in recruitment, promotions and day-to-day operations, ensuring workplace practices.
Globalization: With businesses expanding globally, DEI strategies must adapt to embrace perspectives and practices.	Businesses need to create global DEI strategies that honor and integrate norms and practices promoting inclusivity in all aspects of their business operations.
Mental Health and Well Being: The increasing acknowledgment of health as an aspect of DEI emphasizes the importance of comprehensive well-being programs.	Implement well-being programs that target health issues in diverse populations, fostering a supportive environment that enhances overall employee well-being and efficiency.

Envisioning the Future

Corporate Responsibility: The surge in activism requires organizations to take a stance on issues, signaling a shift toward more value-oriented business approaches.	Organizations should actively participate in causes that are important to their communities and stakeholders embedding social responsibility into their fundamental values and behaviors.
Hybrid and Remote Work: As remote work becomes more common, innovative methods are needed to promote inclusivity and connectivity, within dispersed teams.	Develop plans to uphold and improve inclusivity and team bonding in remote work setups, making sure every team member feels appreciated and part of the team regardless of where they're located physically.

Section 5: Tailoring Training Programs for Upcoming DEI Trends

To effectively navigate these developments, organizations need to adapt their training programs to cultivate a culture that embraces DEI across all levels. This includes establishing measurable objectives for DEI initiatives while ensuring leadership remains accountable (CIO.com, 2023). Implementing strategies for managing change is crucial for embedding diversity, equity and inclusion (DEI) into the fabric of an organization's culture. According to Orange Grove Consulting (2023) and HR Gazette (2023), this necessitates clear communication with all employees.

Organizations should also prioritize eliminating biases and promoting inclusivity through structured training initiatives that tackle the obstacles identified in their DEI assessments. By involving employees in the DEI transformation process and monitoring progress using metrics, companies can ensure that their training efforts align with the evolving landscape of DEI.

To address these shifts, organizations need to overhaul their training programs to equip both leaders and staff with the skills and knowledge for the future. It is essential to concentrate on areas such as cultivating a workforce, nurturing inclusive environments, promoting equity in opportunities, and enhancing cultural awareness.

Areas of Focus	Implications for Practice
Building Cultural Competence	Training programs must include cultural competence modules to empower employees to navigate and appreciate global diversity effectively. This ensures that all team members have access to the tools and resources to achieve the desired effectiveness of DEI efforts, throughout the company.
Enhancing Digital Literacy	As DEI's efforts increasingly leverage technology, it's vital to implement digital literacy programs. This ensures that all employees can utilize technological tools, making DEI initiatives more accessible and effective across the organization.
Promoting Mental Health Awareness	Integrating mental health education into DEI training underscores the significance of the work environment. This helps in creating a workplace where all employees feel supported and appreciated, addressing the challenges encountered by groups.
Encouraging Inclusive Leadership	Leadership development programs should prioritize inclusive leadership approaches that respect diversity and advocate for fairness. This helps organizations develop leaders who champion DEI initiatives, fostering a workplace culture that's more inclusive and fairer.

Section 6: Wrapping up Chapter 8 with a Call to Action

"The unexamined life is not worth living."

— Socrates

As we conclude Chapter 8 by emphasizing the imperative for thinking about DEI training efforts that are globally conscious, we contemplate how DEI continues to evolve over time. Social movements, global events and technological progress all influence the landscape of DEI which is in a constant state of flux.

Consequently, DEI initiatives need to be flexible and adaptable, prepared to incorporate perspectives and respond to changes. For leaders, it's crucial to stay updated on these shifts. Therefore, training programs should be dynamic, integrating viewpoints and cultural competencies that resonate universally. The aim is to nurture an environment that not only adjusts to current trends but also foresees and shapes future developments.

Envisioning the Future

Keep in mind that DEI is a concept. It evolves as our knowledge of the world and its inhabitants deepens. Let this guide mark the beginning rather than the end of your DEI journey. May these closing reflections act as a catalyst, motivating you to embed these insights into your organization's culture and take steps that reverberate globally as you and your organization move from "**Compliance to Community.**"™ #WeNotMe

Key Takeaways	Counterpoints	Rebuttals
Apple's focus on DEI aims to build a welcoming environment, boost representation and ensure responsibility. All of which have played a role in its achievements.	Some detractors believe that excessive attention to DEI might shift the focus away from business goals.	DEI programs improve performance by encouraging creativity and engagement among employees, directly supporting the core business objectives.
Current trends in DEI involve using technology to highlight the importance of considering various intersecting identities and emphasizing the need for inclusivity on a global scale.	Critics question whether technology can effectively address seated biases and cultural complexities within DEI efforts.	When used thoughtfully, technology can help enhance DEI initiatives by identifying and addressing biases, thereby promoting fairer hiring practices and workplace environments.
To adapt to evolving DEI standards, leaders must be proactive in integrating flexibility into their training programs to stay relevant.	There are concerns about DEI initiatives potentially reacting strongly to shifts, resulting in inconsistent implementation practices.	A thinking DEI approach that anticipates trends enables organizations to uphold their values consistently while adjusting strategies to meet changing demands.

DEI goes beyond borders and necessitates training for embracing diversity across various cultural contexts.	The intricacies of global DEI endeavors may pose challenges for organizations, leading them to implement ineffective measures. The landscape of diversity, equity and inclusion is shaped by shifts in society, fluctuations in the economy and political climates, underscoring the importance of resilience and adaptability. Some doubters may argue that the changing nature of diversity, equity and inclusion poses challenges in establishing strategies that consistently yield positive outcomes.	By prioritizing the development of understanding and promoting an environment of inclusivity, companies can successfully navigate the intricacies of diversity, equity and inclusion initiatives.
Social trends, economic fluctuations, and political climates all have an impact on the DEI landscape, emphasizing the need for resilience and adaptability.	Some may argue that the fluid nature of DEI makes it difficult to establish long-term strategies that are consistently effective.	Viewing diversity, equity and inclusion as domains enables organizations to craft strategies that can adapt to societal transformations, over time, ensuring sustained relevance and influence.

References

1. Apple. (n.d.). Diversity. Retrieved from - https://www.apple.com/diversity/
2. Diversity Social. (n.d.). Certification Apple. Retrieved from - https://diversity.social/certification-apple/
3. Engagedly. (n.d.). 5 companies embracing diversity and inclusion through initiatives. Retrieved from - https://engagedly.com/blog/5-companies-embracing-diversity-and-inclusion-through-initiatives/
4. Fast Company. (n.d.). Entrepreneurs share 9 companies with admirable DEI efforts. Retrieved from - https://www.fastcompany.com/90690943/entrepreneurs-share-9-companies-with-admirable-dei-efforts
5. Forbes. (2023, March 7). 4 critical DEI trends to watch in 2023. Retrieved from - https://www.forbes.com/sites/forbeshumanresourcescouncil/2023/03/07/4-critical-dei-trends-to-watch-in-2023/?sh=4236db972f06
6. Forbes. (2022, June 1). Leading a global team: Eight ways to respect cultural differences. Retrieved from - https://www.forbes.com/sites/theyec/2022/06/01/leading-a-global-team-eight-ways-to-respect-cultural-differences/?sh=7a8963e36167
7. HR Exchange Network. (n.d.). Integrating change management in your DEI interventions. Retrieved from - https://www.hrexchangenetwork.com/hr-talent-management/columns/integrating-change-management-in-your-dei-interventions
8. HR Gazette. (n.d.). DEI in the workplace as change management. Retrieved from -
9.

https://hr-gazette.com/dei-in-the-workplace-as-change-management/

10. Loeb Leadership. (n.d.). The future of DEI: Emerging trends and technologies in driving equity and inclusion. Retrieved from -

    https://www.loebleadership.com/insights/the-future-of-dei-emerging-trends-and-technologies-in-driving-equity-and-inclusion

11. Melyssa Barrett. (n.d.). Top companies with robust diversity and inclusion programs. Retrieved from -

    https://melyssabarrett.com/top-companies-with-robust-diversity-and-inclusion-programs/

12. Orange Grove Consulting. (n.d.). How to integrate change management. Retrieved from -

    https://orangegroveconsulting.com/howtointegratechangemanagement/

13. ParadigmIQ. (n.d.). How cultural diversity training can help global companies be more inclusive. Retrieved from -

    https://www.paradigmiq.com/blog/how-cultural-diversity-training-can-help-global-companies-be-more-inclusive

14. People Managing People. (n.d.). Editorial news future of DEI. Retrieved from -

    https://peoplemanagingpeople.com/culture/dei-culture/editorial-news-future-of-dei/

15. RW-3. (n.d.). The importance of global inclusion training. Retrieved from -

    https://www.rw-3.com/blog/the-importance-of-global-inclusion-training

16. RW-3. (n.d.). Six steps to creating inclusive training. Retrieved from -

    https://www.rw-3.com/blog/six-steps-to-creating-inclusive-training

17. Small Business - Chron.com. (n.d.). Cultural diversity training in the workplace. Retrieved from -

https://smallbusiness.chron.com/cultural-diversity-training-workplace-43290.html

18. Social Talent. (n.d.). 9 companies around the world that are embracing diversity. Retrieved from -

    https://www.socialtalent.com/blog/diversity-and-inclusion/9-companies-around-the-world-that-are-embracing-diversity

19. Teambuilding.com. (n.d.). DEI companies. Retrieved from -

    https://teambuilding.com/blog/dei-companies

20. Vantage Circle. (n.d.). Diversity and inclusion trends. Retrieved from -

    https://blog.vantagecircle.com/diversity-and-inclusion-trends/

21. 360Learning. (n.d.). Cultural diversity training. Retrieved from -

    https://360learning.com/blog/cultural-diversity-training/

22. Impactly. (n.d.). Cultural sensitivity training. Retrieved from -

    https://www.getimpactly.com/post/cultural-sensitivity-training

23. Impactly. (n.d.). Cultural diversity training in the workplace. Retrieved from -

    https://www.getimpactly.com/post/cultural-diversity-training-in-the-workplace

24. Impactly. (n.d.). Cultural diversity & sensitivity training. Retrieved from -

    https://www.getimpactly.com/post/cultural-diversity-sensitivity-training

25. CIO. (n.d.). DEI that works: 5 companies reaping the benefits of IT diversity strategies. Retrieved from -

    https://www.cio.com/article/419578/dei-that-works-5-companies-reaping-the-benefits-of-it-diversity-strategies.html

26. CIO. (n.d.). Diversity and inclusion: 8 best practices for changing your culture. Retrieved from -

    https://www.cio.com/article/228581/diversity-and-inclusion-8-best-practices-for-changing-your-culture.html

Conclusion

"Excellence is the best deterrent to racism or sexism."

- Oprah Winfrey

Combining the essence of **"Mastering Inclusive Leadership: Your Blueprint for Success"** with the innovative **#WeNotMe R.A.C.E™ Framework**, offers a comprehensive conclusion to his exploration of DEI in leadership. Both approaches underscore the critical shift from an individualistic, compliance-based mindset to one that values community, collective action, and genuine engagement.

Continuous learning, self-evaluation, and community-focused actions are characteristics of the path towards inclusive leadership. Embracing these principles leads to enhanced outcomes for all, especially marginalized and sidelined individuals. Success stories across industries demonstrate the transformative power of committed DEI strategies, driven by leaders who dare to make a difference.

As you turn this page, remember that the insights, tools, and strategies you've acquired are not just theoretical constructs but a call to action. Implementing your DEI plan with the knowledge from the **R.A.C.E™ Framework** and the **#WeNotMe** ethos sets you on a path to creating a more equitable, inclusive, and thriving workplace. Your leadership can ignite change, inspire others, and contribute to a better tomorrow.

I encourage you to share your journey towards mastering inclusive leadership. Your review can guide others to embrace DEI, fostering a global work environment where everyone feels included, valued, and empowered. Start making your impact today.

Chapter	Key Takeaway	Goal & Approach	Practical Tools & Strategies
Setting the Stage for Inclusive Leadership	Introduction to DEI	Understand DEI's importance	Company success stories; DEI definitions
Developing Self-Awareness	Recognizing biases and emotional IQ	Improve leadership through self-awareness	Self-assessment tools; Emotional IQ improvement methods

Conclusion

Inclusive Team Building	Essentials of a cohesive work environment	Recruitment, onboarding, retention strategies	Mentorship programs; Talent retention tips
Validating Safe Spaces	Importance of psychological safety and open communication	Cultivate safe and open workspaces	Fair policy enforcement; Communication training techniques
Embodying Authentic Leadership	Authenticity in leadership	Lead by example for inclusive decision-making	Authentic leadership training; Inclusive decision-making methods
Recognizing and Navigating Challenges	Overcoming resistance to DEI initiatives	Navigate through skepticism and maintain DEI momentum	Strategies to overcome skepticism; Maintaining DEI efforts
Success Stories and Practical Tools	Real-world DEI success and practical implementation tools	Turn theory into practice for meaningful change	DEI toolkit; Exercises and assessments

Made in the USA
Middletown, DE
28 June 2024